NATIONAL GEOGRAPHIC
KiDS

HOW TO
SPEAK
ANIMAL

A GUIDE TO LEARNING HOW ANIMALS COMMUNICATE

Aubre Andrus &
Dr. Gabby Wild, D.V.M.

NATIONAL GEOGRAPHIC
WASHINGTON, D.C.

CONTENTS

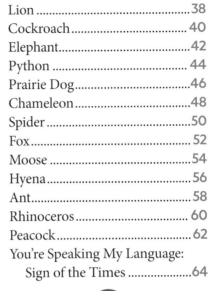

HOW TO USE THIS BOOK

This book is filled with interesting facts about how different animals communicate with the world around them. More than 60 animals are featured, and they are grouped into four sections based on the environments where they are mostly found: on land, in the water, in the air, or living with or near humans. You don't have to read this book in order; you can flip around to find your favorites. But we do recommend that you read Chapter 1, "Communication Basics," first.

In that chapter, we define the key terms you'll need to understand the animal entries later in the book. Then, check out each animal's profile:

ACROSS THE LAND

PRAIRIE DOG

LOCATION: PRAIRIES, GRASSLANDS
PRIMARY COMMUNICATION:

Danger! Danger! This is not a drill.

PRAIRIE DOGS AREN'T **DOGS.** THEY ARE A TYPE OF **RODENT** FROM THE **SQUIRREL** FAMILY.

If a prairie dog from one group meets a prairie dog from another group, there might be a showdown. Each will chatter its teeth, flare its tail, and stare. What are they saying? They are likely trying to prove who is dominant, which can mean the one who is a stronger or better leader.

Although prairie dogs sometimes use visual signals, they are known for their barks. Each bark is slightly different and can provide a lot of information. Different prairie dogs use the same barks, just like different humans use the same words. A bark that's repeated over and over again—at about 40 barks per minute—is an alarm call that warns others of a threat. Different predators—such as badgers, coyotes, or eagles—get different kinds of calls. A "coyote alarm" will send other prairie dogs running. A "badger alarm" will make them crouch down low to hide. In addition to alarm calls, prairie dogs use snarls, growls, and screams when they sense danger.

It's possible that prairie dogs have the most complex language of any animal species on the planet.

That may be because prairie dogs form huge groups—hundreds to thousands can live together in miles of underground burrows, or tunnels. Groups that big need to communicate a lot in order to build, eat, play, protect, and mate.

Say What? PRAIRIE DOG BURROWS are called "towns." The largest known burrow had 25,000 square miles (64,750 sq km) of underground tunnels. It was about the size of the U.S. state of West Virginia and was home to as many as 400 million prairie dogs. Burrows have separate areas for new-born babies, for sleeping, and for going to the bathroom. The average town has 70 entrances. Sometimes other animals, including rabbits and snakes, try to make these burrows their home. But a prairie dog lookout usually stands guard at each entrance to keep these intruders out.

46

• **Name:** Usually we refer to animals by their common name. Animals also have longer scientific names for their genus or species, but those are not included here.

• **Location:** We know that animals are always on the go—yes, even sloths—but instead of listing every single place you could find the animal, we've given their primary habitats. The final chapter, "By Our Side," includes animals that you may find at your house or on a farm. But even for these animals that live with or near people, we've listed their primary habitat in the wild.

• **Primary Communication:** This part of the entry highlights an animal's primary form of communication. We've also listed a secondary or even a third or fourth form when those are also used frequently. The symbols for communication styles look like this:

AUDITORY
HEARING

VISUAL
SEEING

TACTILE
TOUCHING

CHEMICAL
SMELLING/
SENSING

Also look out for these special sidebars throughout the book:

INSIDER INFO

INSIDER INFO gives you even more facts about that animal or related species.

SAY WHAT? offers wacky and unusual information about the animal.

SPEAK UP suggests ways you can get involved to help save or protect this species.

DR. WILD'S WORDS

DR. WILD'S WORDS offers insight from expert veterinarian Dr. Gabby Wild.

To tell you about as many animals as possible, we share key information about each one. Then, at the back of the book, we've included a list of further resources, which is full of ideas for where to find more information. There's also a glossary and an index.

MEET DR. GABBY WILD

VETERINARIAN AND WILDLIFE EXPERT

As a wildlife veterinarian and conservationist, I need to understand how animals communicate in order to protect them, take care of them, and keep myself and our veterinary staff safe when working with them. Mostly, I communicate with animals by speaking to them in a respectful tone as I would with another person. For example, when I examine parrots, I actually talk to them (in English!) and ask them to step up on my hand for an examination. When working with Asian elephants that were once trained for tree logging, I have been able to examine them by using verbal Thai commands and hand signals. I use these specific commands in order to examine their feet, have them turn to the side, and even lift me up so I can better see their back and ears.

After years of research and fieldwork with many different species of animals, scientists and veterinarians like me have started to decode the different forms of communication that species have and use with one another. Some forms are learned, like a dog that is trained to sit, roll over, or play dead. Other animals have some forms of communication that they were naturally born with, such as a baby herring gull pecking at the red spot on his or her parents' beaks. This triggers the parents to regurgitate food for them (gross— I know!).

Some animals communicate through visual cues; for example, zebra mothers walk around their newborn baby calf so the baby can learn to recognize his or her mother's unique stripe pattern. They also "talk" through hormonal cues, such as pheromones—a type of chemical that many animals produce and release into the environment. Wolves, for instance, secrete pheromones from special glands, like the ones between their paw pads, to mark their territory. Some animals also follow auditory cues: Howler monkeys, well, howl

to one another. Their howls can be heard up to three miles (4.8 km) away in the thick rainforest. Still others use tactile communication: Horses kick each other to show aggression!

Recent studies have shown that animals communicate using senses that humans don't even have. Elephants can communicate from great distances using infrasound, which is a wavelength of sound that can't be heard by the human ear. The next time you're at the zoo, you may be lucky enough to catch the elephants communicating in this way with one another—you may even feel their "rumble" vibrating beneath your feet.

Whether you are planning a camping trip, a trip to the zoo or a safari, or a walk in a dog park, I hope this book motivates you to recognize and be inspired by the amazing world of communication across the animal kingdom. By observing a female songbird listening to a male's performance before choosing him as a partner, or a sibling rivalry between spotted hyenas to establish who's in charge, you can discover that animals are not so different from us, even if they "speak" in a way that we may not at first easily understand. Perhaps one day you'll be the one to translate what the animals are saying. Stay wild!

1

COMMUNICATION BASICS

WHY DO WE COMMUNICATE?

A CAT PUFFS UP ITS TAIL and arches its back. A lion roars. Two sea otters rub their noses together. A dog pees on a tree. These are all ways in which animals communicate.

Communication happens when two life-forms—as small as an amoeba or as big as a whale—exchange information. (Exchanging means giving and receiving. It's a swap.) Based on what the message says, those life-forms react or respond. Humans talk to each other using words that are written, signed, or spoken. But this type of language is just one way to communicate. Animals may not have a formal written alphabet like humans do, but they can express themselves and give information in other ways.

Animals communicate for many reasons. The most important reason is survival: to eat, to find a mate, and to avoid predators. But animals sometimes communicate just for fun—to play, like humans do. When it comes down to it, animals communicate in ways that are very similar to what humans do. We have more in common than you think.

A mother can find her babies through smell and sound. That's especially helpful for mothers that have to quickly find their babies within a large group of others that look very similar.

I'm your mother.

Many species have specific alarm calls that warn when a predator is near. A certain call may mean that something dangerous is in the sky, while another call may mean that a predator is moving closer on the ground.

Watch out!

This is my home.

Some animals are very territorial, meaning they protect the area in which they live to keep other animals out. They might do this by standing guard and scaring others away with body language. Or they might mark their territory with their own scent. The scent acts like a boundary, or a fence, to keep other animals away.

Some species that hunt together need to communicate with one another to coordinate their attack. They then signal to their young when it's time to eat.

I'm the boss.

Dinner's here!

Species that live in groups act in ways and make sounds that show who is a leader and who is not. Many of these signals are a way of saying, "I'm in charge" or "I will follow your lead."

Animals find mates to produce offspring and keep the species alive. Animals that are looking for a mate use attention-getting signals involving color, sound, and body language.

I like you.

HUMANS VS. ANIMALS

With human language, we can talk about all kinds of things. We talk about things in the past, the present, or the future. We talk about real objects and imaginary ideas. We combine sounds or hand signals to make words. And we have hundreds of thousands of words to choose from. Sometimes we avoid words and use body language instead: We shrug, sigh, or raise our eyebrows. We can also write, read, draw, and more to express our thoughts and feelings.

The animal world cannot communicate in these exact same ways (with a few exceptions, like body language). While humans communicate for many different reasons, animals are usually reacting to something when they communicate, such as hunger or danger. And when they respond, it's usually in the same way each time. That's different from humans, who have many choices. For example, when humans want to greet each other we can wave with our hand, say hello (in whatever language we speak), share a hug, and more.

HOW ANIMALS COMMUNICATE

If animals don't talk, how do they communicate? They use signals of all kinds. These signals show emotion, transfer information, and act as a response. There are four forms of communication that animals most commonly use: auditory, visual, tactile, and chemical. These look like big words, but don't worry—you probably already know what they mean. A species may use only one form, a combination of several, or even all four.

INSIDER INFO

SOME ANIMALS—such as elephants, dolphins, and ants—live in groups or families. Others live alone, including pandas, platypuses, leopards, and sea turtles. Even animals that live alone can communicate with one another. For example, pandas will leave a scent behind on a tree when they want to leave a message for another panda. You could call it "pee-mail."

AUDITORY

🦻

HEARING

VISUAL

👁

SEEING

Birds chirp. Cats meow. Dolphins click. Animals make sounds, or vocalizations, to signal to one another. These are forms of acoustic, or audio, communication. They are very common in the animal world because sound travels fast. This means the signal can be heard almost immediately by another animal.

The way an animal moves its body can send a visual message for other animals to see. These gestures are a form of body language. For example, a male peacock spreads his tail feathers and shakes them to show off to a female. It's as if he's saying, "Pick me!"

TACTILE

TOUCHING

CHEMICAL

👃

SMELLING/ SENSING

Tactile signals happen when two animals touch one another in some way. It could be through grooming—picking bugs off one another's fur, for example—or cuddling—rubbing their necks against each other or the like. Some animal species use touch to fight with one another and show who has a higher rank.

Animals communicate through pheromones (FEHR-uh-moanz), a chemical they give off that affects the behavior of another animal. Pheromones can be left behind (through pee, sweat, or saliva), and the signal can be picked up hours or days later by another animal.

15

HEAR: AUDITORY COMMUNICATION

Auditory communication is a process that involves making noises—and hearing them. Just like humans, many animal species communicate through vocalizations, a fancy way of saying they make noises. Animals and humans often make these sounds by using their larynx, or voice box. Think about a lion roaring or a wolf howling. This is called verbal communication. Other species, such as crickets, make sounds with their body: They create noise by rubbing their wings together.

Many humans and animals hear these noises with their ears. Sound waves travel through the ear canal, the narrow passageway in your ear. They then hit the eardrum, which vibrates. The vibrations eventually are turned into an electrical signal that goes to your brain. Your brain recognizes this signal as sound. Some animals don't need ears to hear—they can feel the vibrations that a sound gives off.

Some animals communicate with just a few sounds. Others, such as dolphins, monkeys, and chimps, make a wider range of noises. The sounds animals make can be short or long, high or low, and loud or soft. Some can even be described as song-like. Each version of the sound sends a different message. But when it comes to the number of different meanings for sounds, no species comes close to humans: It's estimated that there are about one million words in the English language.

For species in the animal world that need to get someone's attention fast, sound is the most common way to communicate. Sound, especially a loud sound, travels through the air quickly, and it travels a great distance. In the wild, even a few seconds can be the difference between life and death if a predator is nearby. Some animal sounds are too high or low to be heard by humans. It's usually a good thing when animals make noises that humans or other animals can't hear: If an animal can't be heard by its predators, it is less likely to be attacked.

GRAY WOLF

WOLVES' SENSE OF SMELL IS **100** TIMES BETTER THAN HUMANS'.

POISON DART FROG

SEE: VISUAL COMMUNICATION

Your body language says a lot. The most obvious way you can show others what you feel is through your facial expressions, or the way you arrange your face. A big smile or a deep frown can express two very different feelings. Gestures are how you use your hands or limbs—for example, when you wave or give a high five. Posture is how you position your body. Are you standing shoulders back, head up tall and proud, or are you slouched on the couch, relaxed and comfortable? Facial expressions, gestures, and posture are three types of body language that are all visual displays of communication, which means they can be seen. They are also nonverbal, which means they don't require sound or words.

Animals can use these three types of body language to send a silent signal to one another, too. Many animals communicate by changing the position of their ears, their tails, or even their eyes. This is especially helpful to animals that are active during the day, as opposed to nocturnal animals that come out only at night. (Some animals that spend most of their time in the dark either adapted specialized night vision or other ways to communicate.)

Some animals send messages with the coloring of their skin, scales, shells, or feathers. For example, poison dart frogs are very brightly colored. This means that predators can spot them quickly—but it also sends another message. The color acts almost like a stop sign—as a "Do not eat me!" warning signal. It tells the predator that the frog is poisonous or bitter tasting. This use of color as a defense is another kind of visual, nonverbal signal that animals can send and is called aposematic coloration.

Other animals put on displays, such as waving their claws or making a series of dance-like steps. These performances act as a signal to a specific audience. Depending on whether it is seen by a predator, prey, or potential mate, the signal will have a very different meaning.

TOUCH: TACTILE COMMUNICATION

Humans give hugs, high fives, and kisses. But they can also kick, push, and shove. This physical contact, when two people are touching, can have very different meanings. The animal world is no different. Some animals use their bodies to show affection. For example, a mother elephant may wrap its trunk lovingly around its baby. Some animals know how to use their body to show force when they are angry, such as a moose that will charge another animal with its large antlers.

Tactile communication can happen only when two animals are in near proximity, meaning they are physically close, sitting or standing beside each other. They have to be able to reach each other, after all. We see tactile communication most when animals are hanging out together in a group. Some animals, like monkeys, show affection by grooming one another. This "social grooming" is a way for animals to bond. Not only does this grooming help animals keep each other's coats clean, but it also reinforces their friendship.

THE NOSE OF A STAR-NOSED MOLE HAS 22 TENTACLES THAT ENABLE IT TO IDENTIFY 12 OBJECTS PER SECOND.

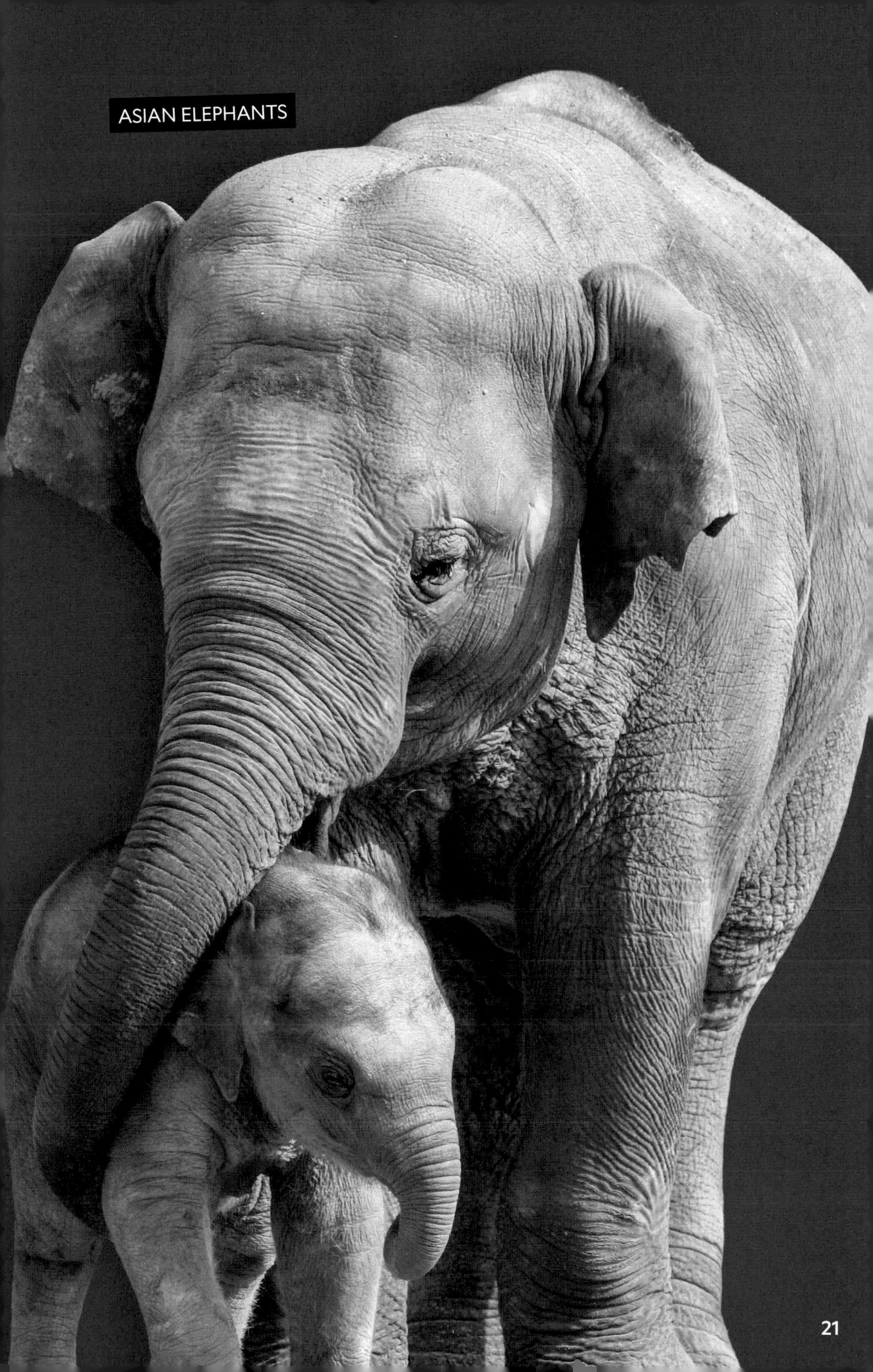
ASIAN ELEPHANTS

SMELL: CHEMICAL COMMUNICATION

Many animals communicate through scents. Every individual animal has a "perfume" or a signature scent, including humans. But animals' noses are often much more sensitive than ours. They can learn a lot of information through scent, even detecting if the scent comes from a predator, prey, or a member of their family. That's much more than humans ever could detect.

These unique scents often come from pheromones. Pheromones are chemicals that are found in such things as spit, pee, mucus, or sweat. Animals can detect the pheromones and then determine what that scent means. Often it's something an animal has left to mark its territory. Marking their territory is a way to tell other animals "Stay away. This is mine." This usually happens through pee. Other animals don't see the pee—they detect the pheromones in the pee. And they know it means they should stay away. That scent may stick around for hours or days, so it's an effective way to communicate with a lot of animals (like any creature that walks by) over a longer period of time.

Pheromones can also be used to give an instant message. Think of a skunk that sprays a stinky odor when a predator gets in its path. It means "Get away!" Other animals might look as if they are touching each other, when in reality it's the pheromones they are after. For example, two dogs that touch noses when they first meet can detect the pheromones in the mucus and the spit that cover the other dog's nose. Smelling that scent is like reading a biography about the other dog.

AS IT SOARS THROUGH THE SKY, AN ALBATROSS CAN SMELL THE FISH THAT ARE SWIMMING IN THE OCEAN FAR BELOW IT.

PET COMMUNICATION

You've probably wondered if you'll ever be able to really talk to your pet. You are not alone. Behavioral scientists, animal trainers, and veterinarians use technology and research to study how animals communicate with one another. And this research has helped humans communicate in a limited way with certain animals. We've learned so much from the work of scientists like Jane Goodall, who lived in the wild and after studying chimpanzees learned how to make some of their calls.

Translating an animal's "language" is a long, slow process. One way that scientists have learned how animals communicate is by recording their vocalizations, playing them back to the animals, and then seeing how they react. For example, if prairie dogs react to a certain call by looking upward and then running away, scientists can figure out that this sound may be an alarm call that signals a predator is nearby.

Scientists are working on inventions that could help us communicate even more clearly with animals. For example, researchers are developing a device that might translate a dog or cat's facial expressions and sounds into words that humans can understand.

Decades of research on wild and domestic animals have helped us to better train our pet cats and dogs today. Animals will never speak humanlike sentences and create the complex messages we do—and that's OK. But when you better understand the body language and sounds your pet makes, you can better understand their wants and needs and react accordingly. That's communication.

READ ON ▷ INTERSPECIES COMMUNICATION, when two different species are able to send messages between each other and understand each other, is complicated. While this book primarily focuses on how animals communicate with each other, there are some ways in which humans have gotten creative and figured out how to communicate with animals:

pp. 64–65: Learn how humans use sign language to communicate with gorillas.
pp. 104–105: Discover how humans are learning to "speak dolphin."
pp. 138–139: Find out whether some birds can really talk to humans.
pp. 166–167: Read about the unspoken language between horses and humans.

2

ACROSS THE LAND

A CONSTANT CHATTER BUZZES across the surface of planet Earth. Much of it comes from the hustle and bustle of humans. But the rest of it is from the animal kingdom. From the largest land animal, the elephant, to the tiniest of ants, and from slow-moving sloths to fast-striking pythons, animals are communicating. As humans, we can't hear it all, we can't see it all, and we don't yet understand it all. But the ability to communicate allows animals to thrive in the forests, prairies, and other environments across the land.

AFRICAN
ELEPHANT

AN **ADULT** MALE **GORILLA** CAN WEIGH UP TO **600 POUNDS** (272 KG).

Listen up—I'm in charge here!

GORILLA

LOCATION: FORESTS, PLAINS, SAVANNAS

PRIMARY COMMUNICATION: 👂 👁 ✋

Instead of fighting with each other when they disagree, gorillas use gestures. They beat their chest with their open hands and make loud hooting noises. Gorillas wrestle, but they aren't fighting. Biting, hitting, and hugging are ways they play with each other. Adult gorillas tend to gently touch baby gorillas—more often than they touch other adults. But adults will also pat or tug each other as if to suggest, "Come with me or "Hello."

Gorillas also communicate by making facial expressions and changing their posture just as humans do. But mostly they communicate by making all kinds of sounds: grunts, whimpers, screams, chuckles, barks, belches, and whines. As the leader of his family, a male gorilla makes the most vocalizations.

When a male gorilla senses danger, he'll make sounds but might also emit a scent. This body odor, which the other gorillas can smell, acts as an alarm and alerts the others to take cover or run away. And it warns predators to "back off!"

HEDGEHOG

LOCATION: FORESTS, SAVANNAS, DESERTS

PRIMARY COMMUNICATION:

To attract a mate, a male hedgehog will circle around a female hedgehog. He may snort and puff as he circles. Sometimes he'll carry on this noisy dance for hours.

Most of the time, hedgehogs are solitary creatures, meaning they prefer to be alone. If another hedgehog approaches, the first will make a click or a popping noise as a warning. If the other hedgehog doesn't leave, the first will charge and butt heads with the other animal.

A hedgehog has 3,000 to 5,000 spines (or hollow, modified hairs) on its back. This hairlike armor is made of keratin, the same material that makes up human fingernails. The spines lie flat on the hedgehog's body until a predator—a fox, for example—comes near. To protect itself, the hedgehog hisses, and its spines stand up. They form a crisscross pattern that make the hedgehog's body sharp and pointy. Then the animal tucks into a ball to protect its soft stomach, head, tail, and legs. In this position, the hedgehog is almost impossible to eat. That's why hedgehogs sleep in this position too.

INSIDER INFO

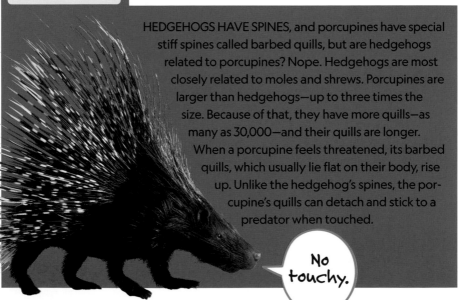

HEDGEHOGS HAVE SPINES, and porcupines have special stiff spines called barbed quills, but are hedgehogs related to porcupines? Nope. Hedgehogs are most closely related to moles and shrews. Porcupines are larger than hedgehogs—up to three times the size. Because of that, they have more quills—as many as 30,000—and their quills are longer. When a porcupine feels threatened, its barbed quills, which usually lie flat on their body, rise up. Unlike the hedgehog's spines, the porcupine's quills can detach and stick to a predator when touched.

No touchy.

IF A **HEDGEHOG** FALLS FROM A TREE, IT CAN PUFF OUT ITS **QUILLS** TO **SOFTEN** THE FALL.

THE
**GOLD
FROG**
IS AS SMALL
AS A **DIME.**

EUROPEAN
TREE FROG

FROG

LOCATION: MOUNTAINS, DESERTS, FORESTS

PRIMARY COMMUNICATION:

The male Brazilian torrent frog makes more gestures than any other frog species. It bobs its head and waves its arms. It wags its toes, stretches its legs, and shakes its hands. Scientists believe this body language has two different meanings, depending on who sees it. If a male sees it, it's meant to scare him away. But if a female sees it, it's meant to impress her.

These same torrent frogs also make a series of noises including peeps and squeals. If a female frog likes what she hears, she'll raise her arm and then touch the male's foot. And that makes him peep some more. His return call is a five-note call.

The Brazilian torrent frog is just one example, but there are more than 4,000 species of frogs. Male frogs (not the females) make sounds to communicate. Have you ever heard frogs *ribbit, ribbit* at night, especially by a pond? This *ribbit,* also called croaking, is the sound that some males make to call to females. Frogs have vocal cords, just like humans do. But they also have a vocal sac, which is like a little pouch on their throat. This sac is inflated with air from the frog's lungs, which can make its noise even louder. Some of these croaks can be heard from one mile (1.6 km) away.

I hope she can hear me ...

TORRENT FROG

Say What? SOME SPECIES OF South American frogs have poisonous skin. These frogs are usually brightly colored with red, yellow, or orange skin. This bright color serves as a warning signal to other animals. It's a way of saying, "Don't eat me!" One species of tiny frog, found in Colombia, is so poisonous an adult human could die just by touching it.

CRICKET

LOCATION: FORESTS, GRASSLANDS, MEADOWS

PRIMARY COMMUNICATION: 👂

You've heard their famous chirps, but did you know that crickets can have a private "conversation"? When crickets produce noise, it's very high-pitched—and for some species of crickets, the sound is higher than any other animal can hear, including humans. This means that crickets can communicate with one another and not worry about any predators, such as bats, hearing them. Just in case, when a cricket senses the vibrations of another animal or person moving closer it will stop making noise so that it won't be found.

Crickets also rub their wings together to chirp. One wing is flat and the other has a comblike structure. When rubbed together they make "music." The process is called stridulation. Crickets hear each other's music through their tiny ears, which are small dots located just below the knees on their front legs.

The crickets you hear chirping at night are male crickets. Female crickets' wings aren't shaped in the same way so they can't make that noise. Males chirp mostly to capture the attention of the females. They'll change the way they rub their wings and create one song for a female that is far away and a different song for one that is close by. They also chirp to keep other male crickets away.

DR. WILD'S WORDS

DID YOU KNOW that you can figure out the current temperature outside by listening to crickets? According to the *Old Farmer's Almanac,* you can count the number of chirps in 14 seconds and then add 40 to calculate the current temperature in Fahrenheit degrees. That's because crickets chirp more often when it's warm outside. As cold-blooded insects, their muscles, including the muscles that help them chirp, move more easily and quickly in warm weather.

Today is a real scorcher!

ALONG WITH **CRICKETS, GRASSHOPPERS** AND **LOCUSTS** ALSO HAVE **EARS ON THEIR KNEES.** THESE ARE THE **TINIEST EARS** IN THE ANIMAL KINGDOM!

GREAT GREEN BUSH CRICKET

SLOTH

LOCATION: CENTRAL AND SOUTH AMERICAN TROPICAL RAINFORESTS

PRIMARY COMMUNICATION:

HOFFMANN'S TWO-TOED SLOTH

Sloths communicate through their poop. Three-toed sloths spend most of their life hanging upside down from a tree, and they come to the ground only about once every eight days to go to the bathroom. They can wait so long because it can take food more than 50 days to move through their body. But scientists believe that a female sloth looking for a mate will climb down from the trees every day for a week and leave poop behind. The scent from her poop helps a mate find her. And she can also sniff around to see if any other mates are nearby.

Sloths also communicate with sound. Two-toed female sloths make a loud *ah-eeeeeh* call in the middle of the night when they are looking for a mate. Any males nearby will come nearer, and scientists believe the males may even fight each other until there is one winner.

Baby sloths make squeaking, peeping sounds when they are alone and need to find their mother. Since adult sloths can't see more than a few feet, these squeaks are an important way to communicate.

A
SLOTH'S
HAIR, WHICH **GROWS**
UPWARD, HELPS
RAINDROPS FALL OFF THE
SLOTH'S BODY MORE
EASILY WHEN IT
HANGS UPSIDE
DOWN.

INSIDER INFO

THREE-TOED SLOTHS are the slowest animals on Earth. They move sluggishly as they climb through the lush trees of tropical forests. And they sleep for up to 20 hours a day. But when they need to, they can quickly slash a hungry boa with their three-inch (7.6-cm)-long claws in defense. Scientists believe that slow-motion body movements are one way that sloths protect themselves. Moving so slowly makes it harder for predators like hawks and eagles to see them. For sloths, slow is a way to survive.

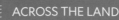

LION

LOCATION: WOODLANDS, GRASSLANDS

PRIMARY COMMUNICATION: 👂 👁 ✋ 👃

Lions are known for their loud roar, but that's not the only way they communicate. They also like to gnaw on one another with friendly, gentle bites. This nibble is actually a form of play. When lions from one pride, or family unit, greet each other, they rub their heads and necks together. This is also how they act when they meet a new lion. As they rub heads and necks, they recognize or learn each other's scents.

When a lion feels threatened, it shows off its sharp teeth. The lion will stand on the tips of its toes, arch its back, and lift its tail to look as big as possible. Lions may also pee or dig with their hind paws to mark their territory. Their paws have scent glands. So when a lion digs or scratches, he leaves behind a scent that tells lions from other prides to stay away. Their loud roar can give this same message.

While a roar is their most well-known call, lions make lots of noises. During play, to show they are comfortable or friendly, they make humming and puffing noises. A puff sounds like a sneeze. A mother lion will meow softly to call to her cubs. Other noises a lion might make include a hiss, grunt, growl, woof, and snarl.

SPEAK UP

AFRICAN LIONS HAVE NO NATURAL PREDATORS, but there still are only about 20,000 left in the wild. They've lost most of their habitat—only 8 percent of it remains. When an animal loses land to human homes, roads, or buildings, it is hard for them to survive. Other wild cat species are threatened with extinction, too. Talk to your teachers or local librarians about researching ways that you can help protect lions and their territories. Look for work done by organizations like National Geographic, the World Wildlife Fund, and the African Wildlife Foundation to find out how you can get involved.

Researchers in Uganda collar a sleeping lion for tracking.

A LION'S
ROAR
CAN BE HEARD FROM
FIVE MILES (8 KM)
AWAY.

39

COCKROACH

LOCATION: MOIST AREAS INDOORS AND OUTDOORS

PRIMARY COMMUNICATION:

Cockroaches have a reputation for being dirty, but they're actually very clean. All through the day, a cockroach grabs its antenna with one of its legs and cleans it with its mouth. Their antennae have tons of pores, or tiny holes, that can detect up to 154 different smells. This regular cleaning keeps the pores of the antennae unclogged, so they can pick up on scent-based messages.

One of these messages tells them where they can find other cockroaches. Their poop is filled with bacteria that has a certain scent. Other cockroaches are attracted to this scent, and it's one reason cockroaches hang out in a group. Sometimes as many as three dozen cockroaches will live together. When cockroaches can't detect this scent, they will live alone.

I smell a party!

The Madagascar hissing cockroach has additional ways to communicate. It forces air through its various breathing holes, producing a hissing noise that scares off predators—or other males. It also uses its body to communicate, by kicking and shoving other males or standing on its toes to look bigger and scare them away.

DR. WILD'S WORDS

ROACHES ARE thigmotropic. This means they like to feel something solid around themselves at all times. They squeeze into cracks and crevices to get this sensation. In fact, cockroaches spend 75 percent of their time like this. Of course, this also keeps them hidden from danger.

IF A COCKROACH'S **HEAD** IS **CHOPPED OFF,** IT CAN STILL MOVE ITS LEGS FOR UP TO A **WEEK LATER.**

HISSING COCKROACH

ELEPHANT

LOCATION: FORESTS, PLAINS, SAVANNAS

PRIMARY COMMUNICATION:

After a group of elephants share a meal, one elephant will lift a leg toward the direction she wants to go and flap her ears. Then she'll make a rumble, which means something like "Let's go!" When an elephant feels intimidated, it will spread its ears wide and lift its head and tusks into the air. These gestures are examples of how elephants use body language to communicate.

Elephants also communicate with one another by making noises. These noises convey messages—guiding a lost elephant toward them or warning other elephants that danger is coming, for example. While known for their trumpet-like call, elephants can make a lot of other sounds: growling, rumbling, roaring, snorting, groaning, crying, and squealing. Humans can't hear all the noises that elephants make, as most of them are too low for our ears to detect. But those low noises are strong and can travel up to five miles (8 km) away.

Elephants like to touch each other lovingly with their trunks. Mothers wrap their trunks around their calf's belly to show affection. Some elephants twist their trunks together to show they are mates. When an elephant is uneasy, it may use its trunk to touch its own face. It's a way for the elephant to self-soothe and make itself feel better.

DR. WILD'S WORDS

ELEPHANTS can communicate using a sound wave called infrasound that is too low for humans to hear. This low-frequency sound travels really far, which is ideal for elephants that need to communicate across long distances. Scientists have learned that these "rumbles" can mean different things, including babies calling out for their mothers, battle cries, alarm calls, greetings, and more.

Let's get ready to rumble!

WHEN ELEPHANTS NOTICE A NEW SCENT, THEY HOLD THEIR TRUNK UP IN AN S-SHAPE.

AFRICAN ELEPHANT

Say What? THE LOW NOISES THAT ELEPHANTS MAKE (the ones that humans can't hear) are more than just noises. These noises also cause vibrations in the ground. Scientists believe that elephants can feel those vibrations through their sensitive trunks, bones, or feet. Tsunamis, which are a series of big waves caused by earthquakes, also send vibrations through the ground. In 2004, elephants in Thailand traveled to a higher ground before a tsunami struck. Scientists believe the elephants felt the vibrations in the ground and could sense that danger was coming. It meant they had to move away from the water to stay safe.

43

A **PYTHON SQUEEZES** SO TIGHTLY AROUND ITS **PREY** THAT IT CAN DETECT THE PREY'S **HEARTBEAT.**

SCRUB PYTHON

44

PYTHON

LOCATION: RAINFORESTS, SAVANNAS, DESERTS

PRIMARY COMMUNICATION: 👁 👃

When pythons feel threatened and are gearing up to attack, they move their body into an S-shaped position. This says, "I will strike." Ball pythons can't move very quickly, so they prefer to sit and wait for prey, such as rodents, to come near. Then they ambush—or surprise—them. They're able to ambush prey by using chemoreception, which means they can recognize chemicals around themselves and decode their meaning. The prey won't even realize it's sending a message to the python until it's too late—lunchtime!

One way that pythons detect a prey's signal is through the heat-sensing pits on their lips. These pits sense temperature changes, which can help the pythons spot nearby warm-blooded prey, such as mammals. Another way is through scent. Although a snake has nostrils, it doesn't actually use them to smell. It uses its tongue to "smell." The snake sticks its forked tongue out of its mouth to pick up scents that are traveling through the air. When it pulls its tongue back in, sensors on the roof of its mouth, called a Jacobson's organ, pick up on these scents. The scent passes along a message to the python's brain, letting it know if it is near predator or prey.

INSIDER INFO

RETICULATED PYTHONS can grow to be more than 30 feet (9 m) long. Unlike humans, however, their skin doesn't stretch and grow as they do. Instead, snakes grow new skin and shed their old skin as many as four times per year. The old layer of skin can come off in one piece.

PEELING SKIN

PRAIRIE DOG

LOCATION: PRAIRIES, GRASSLANDS

PRIMARY
COMMUNICATION:

If a prairie dog from one group meets a prairie dog from another group, there might be a showdown. Each will chatter its teeth, flare its tail, and stare. What are they saying? They are likely trying to prove who is dominant, which can mean the one who is a stronger or better leader.

Although prairie dogs sometimes use visual signals, they are known for their barks. Each bark is slightly different and can provide a lot of information. Different prairie dogs use the same barks, just like different humans use the same words. A bark that's repeated over and over again—at about 40 barks per minute—is an alarm call that warns others of a threat. Different predators—such as badgers, coyotes, or eagles—get different kinds of calls. A "coyote alarm" will send other prairie dogs running. A "badger alarm" will make them crouch down low to hide. In addition to alarm calls, prairie dogs use snarls, growls, and screams when they sense danger.

It's possible that prairie dogs have the most complex language of any animal species on the planet.

That may be because prairie dogs form huge groups—hundreds to thousands can live together in miles of underground burrows, or tunnels. Groups that big need to communicate a lot in order to build, eat, play, protect, and mate.

Say What?

PRAIRIE DOG BURROWS are called "towns." The largest known burrow had 25,000 square miles (64,750 sq km) of underground tunnels. It was about the size of the U.S. state of West Virginia and was home to as many as 400 million prairie dogs. Burrows have separate areas for newborn babies, for sleeping, and for going to the bathroom. The average town has 70 entrances. Sometimes other animals, including rabbits and snakes, try to make these burrows their home. But a prairie dog lookout usually stands guard at each entrance to keep these intruders out.

CHANGING **COLOR** HELPS **CHAMELEONS** **COOL** DOWN OR **WARM** UP. DARKER COLORS **ABSORB** MORE HEAT, WHICH HELPS KEEP THEM WARMER.

PANTHER CHAMELEON

CHAMELEON

LOCATION: RAINFORESTS, DESERTS, SAVANNAS

PRIMARY COMMUNICATION: 👁

When a male veiled chameleon wants to fight another male veiled chameleon, each will brighten the color of their skin. The chameleon that changes color faster and turns the brightest color will be more likely to win. The chameleon that loses the fight will turn a darker color like brown or gray. That says, "Leave me alone."

These color changes also help all chameleons communicate with one another by expressing emotions. Female chameleons use color to tell a male chameleon to come closer (with bright colors) or go away (with dark colors). Depending on its mood, the color of a chameleon's skin can change from yellow to orange to green to turquoise. A chameleon can control the color on 28 different patches on its body to create patterns. Different colors of different body parts signal different messages.

Chameleons have a "resting color" that usually matches the environment they live in. Those that live in rainforests are often green like the leaves, while those that live in the desert are brown like the sand. It's not unusual for the coloring of an animal's fur or skin to blend into its environment, or camouflage, like that. This process keeps the animal safe.

INSIDER INFO

A CHAMELEON'S SKIN IS MADE UP OF MANY LAYERS. The outer scale-like layer is actually transparent, meaning it's see-through. The layers below contain pigments of all different colors. It also includes a layer of crystals, which are like tiny mirrors because they reflect light. When light shines on a chameleon, it passes through the different layers but is then reflected by the crystals. The reflected light forms different colors depending on which pigment is above it. But this pattern can change, loosening at times, which alters the color that appears on the skin of a chameleon. Perceived color changes and brightness occurs more in adult males because both skin layers of crystal-containing cells are fully developed, whereas only the bottom layer is fully developed in females and juveniles.

SPIDER

LOCATION: ALMOST EVERYWHERE ON EARTH EXCEPT THE POLAR REGIONS, THE HIGHEST MOUNTAINS, AND IN THE OCEAN

PRIMARY COMMUNICATION:

Female brown recluse spiders leave a scent on their web when they want to attract a male partner. The male uses the fine hairs that cover his body to pick up on this scent. But how? His sense of touch can also "read" different chemical substances. It's called a chemotactic sense.

Spiders are known to eat other spiders. So once a male locates a female, he can't just approach her—she'll eat him! To avoid getting eaten, male spiders have to use body language to announce their arrival. The male does a special dance: moving his body, waving his legs, posing in specific positions, and tugging at her web. This way she knows he's a potential mate, not a potential meal.

Spiders build webs to catch prey, attract mates, and communicate with the world around them. They can pluck their webs like a guitar, then translate the sound vibrations it makes. They can also pick up messages about what kind of prey is caught in their web and important information about nearby mates.

INSIDER INFO

SPIDERS ARE NOT CONSIDERED INSECTS. In fact, spiders eat insects. Spiders are in the arachnid family with scorpions and ticks. Insects are part of the Insecta class, which includes butterflies, ants, and beetles. Insects have a body made of three parts, six legs, two antennae, and impressive compound eyes. Spiders have a body made of two parts, eight legs, no antennae, and simple eyes.

GARDEN SPIDER

DARWIN'S
BARK SPIDER

THE
STRONGEST
NATURAL FIBER
IN THE **WORLD** IS
**SPIDER
SILK.**

BROWN RECLUSE
SPIDER

FOX

LOCATION: FORESTS, GRASSLANDS, MOUNTAINS, DESERTS

PRIMARY COMMUNICATION:

When foxes see each other for the first time, they make a *wow, wow, wow* noise. One of the foxes will crouch low but turn up its muzzle. This body language combined with this noise sends a message similar to "I come in peace." Foxes make all kinds of noises to communicate with each other: barks, growls, howls, whimpers, shrieks, and yips. Their calls range from a high-pitched hooting that sounds like an owl to a howling scream to a quieter "gekkering," which sounds like *ack-ack-ack.* Adult foxes that know each other will make whimpering or whining noises. When adults greet baby foxes, known as kits, they make a huffing sound. The most common fox, the red fox, can make 28 different sounds.

Foxes also use scent to send a message. They pee on trees and rocks as a way to say to other foxes, "I'm here now" or "This is my home." In addition, they use their bushy tails to signal to one another and to leave scents behind. The scent gland on their tail actually smells similar to violets. This floral scent can confuse predators, including humans. But foxes don't always smell like flowers—they can also release a stinky scent that humans often confuse for a skunk.

Say What? IN 2013, a Norwegian song called "The Fox (What Does the Fox Say?)" went viral. In the song, the two singers make silly guesses about what noise a fox makes. Of course, scientists do know something about how foxes communicate. But most people are unfamiliar with fox calls because they are unusual and because foxes make many sounds, not just one.

FOXES ARE THE ONLY MEMBER OF THE DOG FAMILY THAT CAN **CLIMB TREES** AND **RETRACT** THEIR CLAWS.

So little time, so much to chat about!

RED FOX

MOOSE

LOCATION: FORESTS

PRIMARY COMMUNICATION:

Moose move their antlers as a form of body language. Different positions can mean different things. When a moose wants to threaten another moose, he lowers his head with his antlers pointed forward. Male moose, called bulls, have impressive antlers that can grow to up to six feet (1.8 m) wide. Bulls use these as a shield against predators and as a weapon to fight other bulls.

During the mating season in the fall, bulls dig a shallow pit with their sharp hooves. They pee in it and then splash the mud-pee mixture onto their antlers and back. Then they lay in the pit to make sure the scent has really covered their body. It's their way of attracting female moose, called cows.

Moose also use sounds to communicate. With large ears that can be rotated 180 degrees, they can hear very well. Bulls make barking sounds, roars, and low croaks. A cow wails when she wants to get the attention of a male, while bulls make a whining sound as a greeting.

INSIDER INFO

MOOSE SHED THEIR ANTLERS EVERY WINTER, and each spring they grow a new pair. Antlers can weigh up to 60 pounds (27 kg), so losing this weight helps them store energy during the cold winter months. As a bull gets older, his antlers will increase in size. Antler bone can grow as fast as eight inches (20.3 cm) in nine days.

MOOSE **BATTLE** EACH OTHER FOR HOURS AT A TIME. THE **CLASHING** OF THEIR **ANTLERS** CAN BE HEARD UP TO **ONE MILE** (1.6 KM) AWAY.

LIKE **DOGS**, **HYENAS** WILL **SNIFF** EACH OTHER'S **REAR ENDS** TO **GREET** EACH OTHER.

HYENA

LOCATION: SAVANNAS, MOUNTAINS

PRIMARY COMMUNICATION:

The spotted hyena makes a giggling noise that sounds like a human laugh. Also known as the "laughing hyena," this animal can make 11 different calls. It's nothing to laugh about, though—this giggle helps hyenas to survive. Their laughter sends multiple messages, from fear to excitement, as well as information about who they are. Hyenas change the pitch to indicate how old they are, and they change the frequency to show how high they rank in their group. Laughter can also be a call for help, especially if a predator, such as a lion, is nearby.

Spotted hyenas live in groups called clans, which can have up to 80 members. They hunt animals together, including zebras, warthogs, and rhinos. This requires a lot of group communication with whoops, groans, squeals, grunting, and growling— especially after the attack as they fight over their catch.

Knowing which rank a hyena is in the clan's pecking order helps decide who gets to eat first.

Hyenas also use body language to communicate. When the striped hyena feels threatened, the hair on its mane stands up, so it looks bigger than it really is. This is meant to intimidate, or scare, its opponent. In hyena clans, the females are dominant, which means they are the leaders. Hyenas communicate this order through body language, such as when the males bow to the females.

I crack myself up!

ANT

LOCATION: DESERTS, BEACHES, AND
EVERYWHERE IN BETWEEN

PRIMARY
COMMUNICATION:

DR. WILD'S WORDS

nts send messages via their antennae, which are two long feelers on top of their heads. That's why ants often touch antennae when they meet. Their entire bodies, including their antennae, are covered with a scented waxy substance that tells them everything they need to know about each other. They learn information such as what that other ant's rank is and what jobs it should be doing to help the colony. Some ants are workers that keep the colony clean and care for the young. Other soldier-like ants fight off intruders and move big objects.

Communication keeps ant colonies organized. Ants release pheromones, the scented chemicals that send various messages. These messages can tell the other ants where to find food or warn that an intruder is nearby. Ants can leave pheromones behind them as they walk, which is why you'll see ants marching in a perfect line. Ants "read" these chemical messages through their antennae.

ONE KIND OF leaf-cutter ant communicates using two pheromones. They place these scents along branches and twigs to signal other ants to come help forage. These chemicals are produced in the poison gland and work best for long-distance communication. For shorter distances, the ants beckon their fellow worker ants using a type of stridulation, which is a form of vibration that alerts other workers where the best leaves are. These vibrations are made when the ants raise and lower their gasters (a part of their abdomen). In other words, this is like an ant booty shake.

ANTS CAN CARRY **50 TIMES** THEIR OWN **BODY WEIGHT.**

WEAVER ANTS

Say What? THE LARGEST ANT COLONY EVER FOUND was more than 3,700 miles (5,955 km) wide. Billions of Argentine ants from 33 different ant populations were living in it. This supercolony was uncovered by scientists along the Mediterranean coast of Europe in 2000.

A NOW **EXTINCT ANCESTOR** OF THE **RHINO,** CALLED **PARACERATHERIUM,** WAS 25 FEET (7.6 M) LONG AND 18 FEET (5.5 M) TALL, WHICH MAKES IT THE **LARGEST** LAND MAMMAL EVER KNOWN.

WHITE RHINOCEROS

RHINOCEROS

LOCATION: GRASSLANDS, FLOODPLAINS

PRIMARY COMMUNICATION:

Rhinos mark their territory with pee, but they send messages to each other with poo. Groups of rhinos create communal dung heaps, or big piles of everybody's poo. By smelling the pile of poo, rhinos can pick up information about other rhinos, including their age and gender. Leaving poo behind is like leaving a message for someone to read later. When rhinos know this information about each other, they won't fight.

When a male rhino wants to attract a mate, he makes a *hic-pant* noise. He inhales air and then hiccups. That's not the only noise he makes—in fact, rhinos' primary communication style is auditory. Other noises they use to communicate include a squeak that means "I'm lost!" and snorts that mean a rhino is angry. When rhinos are content, they will make a deep *mmwonk* noise. During a fight, they'll make a lion-like growl or elephant-like trumpet.

If an animal enters a rhino's territory when it isn't invited, some rhinos will open their mouth and expose their tusks, which look like big pointed teeth. Not all rhino species have tusks, but they do all have one or two horns, which can be used as weapons.

INSIDER INFO

RHINOS LIKE TO BE ALONE, but they allow a bird called the oxpecker to perch on their backs. It's a symbiotic relationship, which means the two animals help each other out. The bird eats parasites such as ticks that live on the rhino's skin. This relationship keeps the rhino clean from pests and provides the bird a meal. Win-win!

BLACK RHINOS AND RED-BILLED OXPECKERS

ONLY **MALES** ARE CALLED **PEACOCKS.** **FEMALES** ARE CALLED **PEAHENS.** TOGETHER THEY'RE CALLED **PEAFOWLS,** AND THE BABIES ARE NAMED **PEACHICKS.**

PEACOCK

LOCATION: LOWLAND TROPICAL FORESTS

PRIMARY COMMUNICATION:

Male Indian peacocks fan out their bright tail and then strut and shake their tail feathers 26 times per second. It's like a dance. This shaking sends out vibrations, which are sensed by the feathered crest of the female. It's a low-pitched mating call that literally rattles her head to get her attention. She not only sees the male's communication, but she feels it. Peafowl can sense vibrations like these that humans can't hear.

When an Indian peacock puts on a semicircle spread of blue, green, and gold, he's looking for a partner through body language. His feathers—which can grow to six feet (1.8 m) long—will impress a female. Females are brown instead of colorful so that they blend in with bushes. This keeps them camouflaged and safe while they protect their eggs.

Indian peacocks also communicate by making hooting and shrill screaming noises that make up 11 different calls. They call mostly during the early morning—and they are loud. These noises may attract other peacocks or can warn others of danger.

SIGN OF THE TIMES

Since the 1930s, scientists have been trying to communicate with great apes. But in 1966, psychologist Dr. Beatrix Gardner and her husband, Dr. R. Allen Gardner, started some research never seen before. They came up with the idea to teach a chimpanzee American Sign Language (ASL). Washoe, the 10-month-old chimpanzee that they adopted to live in their home, learned how to sign hundreds of words.

After Washoe's success, other scientists wanted to try. In the early 1970s, animal psychologist Dr. Penny Patterson began training a one-year-old western lowland gorilla named Koko. She started by teaching Koko a few words in sign language such as "food," "drink," and "more." Patterson said the word as she demonstrated the sign to Koko. Within a few weeks, Koko was combining signs, like "more food." Koko went on to learn about 1,000 signs at the same pace a human child would. And she could understand more than 2,000 spoken English words.

Koko lived with a younger gorilla named Michael that Patterson also taught to understand ASL. The two gorillas were able to sign to each other. They could string together up to eight signs in a row to "speak" more complicated sentences. Sometimes Koko and Michael would create their own signs. For example when Koko signed "finger" and "bracelet," she meant "ring." When Michael signed "more" and "cat" he meant "lion."

Other scientists tried to see if there were other ways to communicate with primates. Kanzi, a bonobo, learned how to point to symbols that represented words. Starting in the 1980s when he was just an infant, scientists taught him that the symbols stood for objects, activities, and concepts like "bad." This was how he was able to communicate with humans. He now uses 348 symbols to form simple sentences and can understand more than 3,000 spoken English words. Scientists believe Kanzi communicates at the same level as a three-and-a-half-year-old human. He lives in the United States at the Ape Cognition and Conservation Initiative in Des Moines, Iowa.

THE GARDNERS WORK WITH WASHOE IN 1976.

KOKO PRACTICES THE SIGN FOR "MACHINE."

3

IN THE WATER

S O MANY SIGNALS SWIM THROUGH the dark, deep ocean, skim the surface of your local pond, or glide along the frozen edges of sea ice. Aquatic, or water-based, species have different ways of communicating than we humans do. After all, they spend much of their time underwater, where a verbal language such as ours can't always be heard. Certain underwater species have developed incredible ways of using sound to communicate through the water. Some change the color of their skin. Others send a message by peeing. Even the slow-moving sea stars have figured out a way to get each other's attention.

MACARONI
PENGUIN

DOLPHIN

LOCATION: OCEANS, SEAS, RIVERS

PRIMARY COMMUNICATION:

Every dolphin has a signature whistle that helps other dolphins identify who they are. It's almost like a name. When a dolphin makes its signature whistle, it's as if it's saying, "Here I am!" It's a way for dolphins in a pod to keep track of one another. Sound travels through water almost five times faster than it does through air, so it's a useful way for marine animals to communicate. If a baby dolphin gets separated from its mother, the two will whistle back and forth until they find each other. Dolphins can memorize each other's whistles and imitate them. Some scientists believe this may be one way they can get each other's attention.

Although dolphins mostly use sound to communicate in dark, murky waters, they will use body language when they are close to one another. Scientists have watched dolphins perform gestures like jumping out of the water when they are playing or slapping their tail on the surface of the water to warn other dolphins of nearby danger. Some also communicate through touch. Dolphins can be seen swimming "holding hands" (fins). They will also ram into each other at full force when they're angry.

INSIDER INFO

DOLPHINS ARE KNOWN FOR BEING VERY SOCIAL ANIMALS—that means they like being around each other. Scientists believe dolphins are as smart as chimpanzees and dogs—if not smarter. All three species can learn to perform certain actions, like tricks, especially when they are given food or other rewards. Dolphins can recognize themselves in a mirror, develop friendships, learn how to understand sign language, and play games.

SPINNER DOLPHINS

Watch this—I'm gonna do a flip!

Show-off ...

DOLPHINS CAN **JUMP 25 FEET** (7.6 M) HIGH ABOVE THE **WATER** AND **SWIM** AT SPEEDS OF UP TO **25 MILES** AN HOUR (40 KM/H).

A CROCODILE'S **170 TEETH** ARE REPLACED OFTEN. IT MAY GO THROUGH AS MANY AS **8,000 TEETH** IN ITS LIFETIME.

CROCODILE

LOCATION: SALTWATER SWAMPS, ESTUARIES

PRIMARY COMMUNICATION:

Special sensors on a crocodile's skin act like motion detectors. More sensitive than a human fingertip, these sensors can detect the ripples of a single droplet, which help the crocodile "feel" the world around it. How is this communicating? Prey move near the crocodile (sending out a signal without even realizing it) and the crocodile responds—that's communicating. These sensors are especially helpful when crocs are searching for prey in muddy, swampy waters.

Adult crocodiles also communicate by making loud, low roars back and forth to other crocodiles. Scientists aren't sure what these mean, but they have figured out that crocs make grunting noises when they want to help their babies and hissing noises when they want to protect their babies from danger.

Crocodiles mostly hang out alone, but sometimes they help each other hunt for food. Within crocodile family groups, each croc has a rank. Lower-ranking crocodiles (which are often smaller) greet more dominant crocodiles (which are often larger) by lifting their snouts. Scientists call this an appeasement behavior, because the lower-ranked animals are trying to keep the peace. If a crocodile prefers to be alone, it will slap its head down loudly onto the water to protect its territory. It may also snap its jaws on the surface of the water.

INSIDER INFO

CROCODILE OR ALLIGATOR?
How can you tell the difference? Here are some distinct features to help you tell crocs and alligators apart: If you see a sharp tooth sticking out from the bottom jaw, it's a crocodile. A U-shaped snout, as opposed to a V-shaped one, likely belongs to an alligator. If they're swimming in salt water, it's probably a croc because alligators live in freshwater.

ALLIGATOR

OCTOPUS

LOCATION: OCEANS

PRIMARY COMMUNICATION: 👁

MIMIC OCTOPUS

When an octopus wants to fight another octopus, it turns a dark color. If the octopus it confronts stays the same color, or matches its dark color, then it's as if that octopus is saying, "Let's fight!" But if the second octopus turns a paler color, it's a way of saying, "I don't want to fight."

However, octopus fights don't happen often. Scientists believe body language is one of the ways that octopuses avoid fighting. After all, they are often found living alone. A dark, angry octopus stands tall with its tentacles spread, while a pale, scared octopus crouches low.

Octopuses try to avoid fights with other animals, too. They can change their color and body shape instantly to hide from predators or to sneak up on prey without it noticing. They can blend into the background by matching any color, pattern, or texture. They can even change their shape to look like a shell or a rock, complete with bumps and ridges. One species, the mimic octopus, will alter itself to look and behave like other sea creatures, such as a sea snake, to escape a predator.

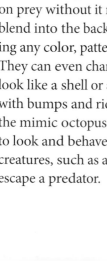

OCTOPUSES HAVE **EIGHT ARMS,** **THREE HEARTS,** AND A DOUGHNUT-SHAPED **BRAIN.**

COMMON OCTOPUS

SEA LION

LOCATION: OCEANS, SEAS

PRIMARY COMMUNICATION:

Say What? SEA LIONS LIVE onshore near water. They are often found hanging out in marinas or lounging on docks, buoys, and even in boats. In San Francisco, California, U.S.A., the K dock at Pier 39 is filled with sea lions. One arrived in 1989, right after the area was struck by an earthquake. Within months, there were more than 300 hanging out there. At times, as many as nearly 2,000 sea lions have called the K dock home. Because of them, Pier 39 has become a tourist attraction. So while they may be loud and stinky, they are also sea-lebrities!

When a mother sea lion wants to find her baby, called a pup, she makes a loud trumpet noise. The pup recognizes her voice and responds with a bleating noise that the mom identifies. Once they find each other, the mother will smell the pup as a final check to make sure she's got the right one.

Sea lions are known to be chatty. They make loud barks, honks, grunts, and growls. They live in groups that can range from a few hundred to a few thousand. When they all talk at once, it gets noisy. A group of sea lions can sound like a group of overexcited barking dogs.

Male sea lions protect the females and the pups from predators or other male sea lions that aren't a part of their family. The males bark or roar to scare intruders away. They can even make these noises underwater. Their ears may be small, but they can hear well both above and below the water. They also use body language like head shaking and lunging forward to show how strong they are. If a sea lion wants to peacefully greet another sea lion, it will rub whiskers with it.

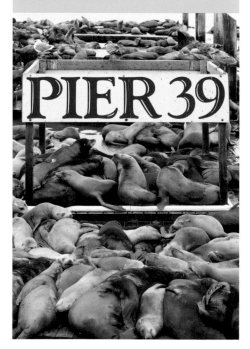

Where are you, pup?! Get your flippers over here this instant!

DR. WILD'S WORDS

SOME AQUATIC MAMMALS have adaptations that allow them to see both above and under the water. It's called emmetropia—aka "no blurriness." Each species has a very specific pupil shape that can regulate, or control, the amount of light entering the eye. Light hits the retina, which has specialized receptor cells that identify an image. Pinnipeds (seals, sea lions, and walruses) have one area of specialized cells on the retina that allows for "best vision." Some pinnipeds also have the ability to change the shape of their corneas, which is the outer layer of the eye, to help them see clearly.

75

CORAL CAN ABSORB **NUTRIENTS** FROM **FISH PEE,** WHICH HELPS THE **REEF GROW.**

CICHLID FISH

LOCATION: OCEANS

PRIMARY COMMUNICATION:

The cichlid fish uses its pee to send messages. It's true—fish really do pee. They have a tiny rear opening called a "pore" from which they urinate (pee). They pee in pulses, or short bursts. The chemicals in the pee send a message to "back off." Cichlid fish are territorial, which means they like to protect their home and don't like any other unwanted guests. So when one encounters a rival, whichever fish pees the most is considered the dominant fish, or the winner of the fight. Once the two fish have exchanged this message, the subordinate fish, or the lesser fish that has lost the fight, will quiver its fin and swim away.

Scientists weren't sure if fish could send messages through urine until a 2017 study from the University of Bern in Switzerland found the proof. In order to see the fish's urine in the water, scientists injected cichlid fish in a tank with a bright blue dye. When the fish peed, the urine was blue. That allowed the scientists to see it and also to measure how much the fish peed.

A **SEA STAR** CAN **REGENERATE,** OR **REGROW,** A MISSING ARM.

COMMON
BRITTLE STAR

SEA STAR (STARFISH)

LOCATION: OCEANS

PRIMARY COMMUNICATION:

In some species of sea star, the entire body glows as a way to attract a mate. They do this with bioluminescence, a chemical process that creates light energy within the body of a living thing. It's more common to find bioluminescence in sea stars that live in the dark depths of the ocean than in the sea stars found in shallow waters. There are at least 1,600 species of sea stars. In the very deep, dark waters of the Arctic the whole body of some species glows, while elsewhere the animals give off only a short flash of bioluminescent light.

Scientists originally thought that sea stars that live in pitch-black waters don't have eyes. But a 2018 study found that 12 of 13 different species that live in the deep seas of Greenland have eyes. This means they can see the bioluminescence, and scientists reasoned that these light signals are a way to get another sea star's attention as well as to find their way in the dark.

INSIDER INFO

SEA STARS HAVE one very small eye at the end of each point, or arm, on its underside. It looks like a tiny dot. They can bend the tip of their arm to raise the eye and see upward. They can't see colors or see very far or clearly. But they can see a little bit even in the dark ocean. This helps them stay close to the coral reef, which is where they find food to survive.

EYE

BABY **SEA TURTLES** **HATCH** ON SANDY BEACHES, BUT THEY **QUICKLY SCURRY** TO THE **OCEAN**, WHERE THEY LIVE FOR THE REST OF THEIR LIVES.

GREEN SEA TURTLE

SEA TURTLE

LOCATION: OCEANS AND COASTS

PRIMARY COMMUNICATION:

Just before baby sea turtles hatch, they make noises like clicks, hoots, and clucks—but the sounds are so low that many humans can't hear them. However, the nearly hatched siblings in nearby eggs can easily hear one another's calls, which helps them hatch at the same time. As a group, the hatched babies then head to the sea. (Sometimes there are dozens of hatchlings, and at other times there are 100 or more.) Scientists discovered in the 2010s that as the hatchlings head toward the shore, female turtles are calling to them from underwater. These calls help direct the babies to safety in the water. Scientists originally thought only land-dwelling tortoises could vocalize and that their webbed-footed cousins were silent, but now they know differently.

Keeping hatchlings safe is not the only reason sea turtles communicate underwater. Thousands of turtles migrate, or travel, together hundreds of miles every two to three years to the same beach to lay their eggs and bury them under the sand. To coordinate such an organized migration, the turtles communicate with low-pitched calls. Humans usually can't hear these calls either.

TURTLES EAT JELLYFISH. Unfortunately, plastic bags that end up floating in the ocean can look a lot like jellyfish. When a sea turtle mistakenly eats a plastic bag, it can upset its buoyancy—the ability to sink and float—or worse. Scientists estimate that more than 50 percent of sea turtles have eaten a plastic bag. This poses a real threat to the species. You can help turtles by volunteering at a river or ocean cleanup in your area and by avoiding plastic bags and other single-use plastic items.

GREAT WHITE SHARK

LOCATION: COASTAL OCEANS

PRIMARY COMMUNICATION: 👁 👃

When a great white shark opens and closes its mouth, it means that it feels uneasy. It's not a vocalization—no sound is emitted. Shark species cannot vocalize. Instead, the movement is the message. This is just one form of body language that great white sharks use to communicate. Their body language sends other signals as well. If a great white shark arches its back, it's annoyed. If it lowers its fin, it's about to start swimming fast. If it exposes two-thirds of its body into the air then belly flops onto the ocean surface, it's trying to attract attention from a mate. (It's quite unusual for other shark species to raise their head out of the water like this.)

Like other fish, sharks can smell underwater. Their nostrils are used to smell, but not to breathe. That's what their gills are for. Great whites are often solitary creatures, meaning they like to be alone. So they need this sense of smell to communicate with others that aren't nearby. Female sharks release pheromones that are a way of saying, "I'm over here!" Male sharks use their sense of smell to detect the pheromones and find their mate.

 Say What? SWELL SHARKS AND CHAIN CATSHARKS, two species of deep-sea sharks, have brown skin. Yet they sometimes look green. That's because they look like they glow in the dark through a process called biofluorescence. In this process, the animal's skin absorbs light (in this case, the blue light of the ocean) and reemits it as a different color (in this case, neon green). The shark's skin has a mix of light and dark patches, but only the light patches glow green. The resulting pattern helps sharks identify each other.

a chain catshark glowing under UV light

GREAT
WHITE SHARKS
CAN DETECT A FEW
DROPS OF BLOOD
UNDERWATER FROM
UP TO THREE MILES
(5 KM) AWAY.

DR. WILD'S
WORDS

ALL LIVING ANIMALS PRODUCE AN ELECTRIC CURRENT. Sharks rely on special organs called the ampullae of Lorenzini to help them hunt prey, using these currents. The ampullae of Lorenzini can be seen as small black dots located on a shark's head. These dots connect the little pores on the shark's skin through insulated, tubelike canals to a round sac where special receptor cells are located. These cells detect the electric current that comes from the prey. Signals are then sent to the shark's brain, alerting the shark to exactly where its prey is located.

RIVER OTTER

LOCATION: RIVERS, SEAS

PRIMARY COMMUNICATION:

River otters can leave behind a scent marking, or strong odor, by rolling on the ground or rubbing an armful of leaves across their body. They may also pee or poo, leaving a scent. Their poo is sometimes called spraint. Each otter has a unique odor, so these scent messages tell other otters their identity, gender, whether they are looking for a mate, and how long it's been since they've left the scent behind. Scent can also be used to mark their territory. This scent message comes from a gland near the base of the otter's furry tail.

Depending on the species, otters can make as many as 22 different vocalizations. They scream when they are excited. They coo when they interact with one another. Otters also shriek when they are disturbed. Other sounds include barks, growls, whistles, moans, chirps, and snarls.

Otters are best known for being playful. They twist, turn, dive, and slide around in mud, snow, and water. This helps strengthen their bond with each other. It's a way of saying, "I like you." And it's an important part of their communication that scientists believe is helpful in the mating and hunting processes.

Say What? OTTERS ARE BUOYANT, which means they can float. But sea otters are a little more buoyant than river otters, so sea otters actually sleep on their backs while floating on the water. Mother otters will hold the paws of their babies, called pups, as they sleep so they don't drift apart. Sea otters also use kelp, which is seaweed that grows from the bottom of the ocean floor, as an anchor. They wrap it around their bodies to stay in place.

Floaty snuggles!

NORTH AMERICAN **RIVER OTTERS** CAN STAY **UNDERWATER** FOR UP TO **EIGHT** MINUTES.

DURING
BATTLE, A
PORCELAIN CRAB
CAN DETACH ITS
**PINCHING
CLAW**
FROM ITS BODY AND
RUN AWAY.

FIDDLER CRAB

CRAB

LOCATION: LAGOONS, ESTUARIES, TIDE POOLS

PRIMARY COMMUNICATION: 👁 👂

When coconut crabs leave their burrows, they'll wave their claws in the air. This lets other crabs know, "I'm coming. Stay back." Or "Leave me alone." It turns out that these crabs are, well, crabby. They don't like company.

Crabs that live mostly on land, like the fiddler crab, wave their claws around, too. Male crabs do this when they are trying to get the attention of a female crab. They'll also drum with their claws or tap the ground with their legs once they see a female close by. This sound can also be used as a warning signal to other crabs to let them know a predator is nearby.

Like crickets, crabs make noises by rubbing their limbs together in a process called stridulation. They have special ridges on their claws that help make this noise. But ghost crabs can make noises without moving their claws. They use their stomachs. The gastric mill, a part of the stomach that grinds food, can be used to make a growling sound. This growl scares off predators and keeps the crab's claws free in case it needs to attack.

INSIDER INFO

CRABS ARE AMPHIBIOUS, which means they are suited for life on land and in water. Not only can they hang out in both environments, they can easily breathe in both. Crabs use gills like a fish when living in the ocean. As long as these gills stay damp when they're on land, they can breathe just fine. That's why you'll find land-based crabs near tide pools or in damp, dark places.

SALLY LIGHTFOOT CRABS

POLAR BEAR

LOCATION: ARCTIC SEA ICE

PRIMARY COMMUNICATION:

When male polar bears want to fight, they'll let each other know by "mouthing" each other, which is a gentle bite on the face and neck. Then they stand up on their hind legs and push with their strong forepaws. This posture signals that they are ready to rumble. Most of the time, this fighting is just for fun, but sometimes it is to let the other bears know which bear is the most dominant.

Polar bears often wander alone across great distances. As they travel, they leave behind scents with each footprint. These footprints help polar bears find one another. When a polar bear stumbles upon tracks, it can tell whether the footprints belong to another bear they'd like to meet or one they'd like to avoid.

When polar bears spend time together, they make a lot of noises. If you hear an adult hissing, growling, and chomping its teeth, you'll know it's mad. But a polar bear cub that's making noises might not necessarily be angry. Their lip smacking, braying, and chuffing might just be an attempt to get their mother's attention. And if a female polar bear is making chuffing noises, she's probably warning her cubs about a problem. She may even get physical and use tactile communication, using her muzzle or paws to push her cubs away from danger.

SPEAK UP

BECAUSE OF GLOBAL WARMING, sea ice in the Arctic has begun to melt and break apart more quickly than ever before. When the sea ice breaks, the scented tracks that polar bears leave behind for each other are broken up as well. If polar bears can't follow these tracks, they can't find mates. To protect the future of polar bears, we will all have to work together to fight climate change.

CUTTLEFISH

LOCATION: SHALLOW OCEAN WATERS

PRIMARY COMMUNICATION:

When a male cuttlefish is looking for a mate, it changes from black or brown to bold zebralike stripes within seconds. A less dominant male even changes color to secretly look like a female. He'll display female patterns, which are a mottled camouflage made of multicolored splotches, on the side of his body that faces another male; he'll display zebra stripes on the side that faces a female. This way, he can attract the female without drawing attention from a nearby male that would likely want to fight him. The color and pattern of the cuttlefish's skin are mostly controlled by its muscles, which flex, changing the millions of pigment (color) cells in its skin.

Color is just one kind of visual communication that cuttlefish use. When a cuttlefish sees its next meal swimming nearby, in addition to changing color it waves the eight short arms that surround its mouth. It is sending the message "Come here" or something similar. This visual display mesmerizes its prey until the cuttlefish can quickly grab it with one of the two longer tentacles it has hiding below. Their appendages are also used to intimidate other sea creatures. Cuttlefish can spread their arms wide to look bigger. It's their way of saying, "Don't mess with me."

Cuttlefish are relatives of squids and octopuses under the class Cephalopoda. Similar to an octopus (pp. 72–73), they can shoot a burst of dark brown ink, called sepia, at predators. They can also change the texture of their skin from smooth to rough so they blend into the sand or rocks of the seafloor.

WHEN **CUTTLEFISH** MOVE FROM A **DARKER** LOCATION TO A **LIGHTER** ENVIRONMENT, THEIR **PUPILS** CHANGE FROM A CIRCULAR SHAPE TO A **W-SHAPE.**

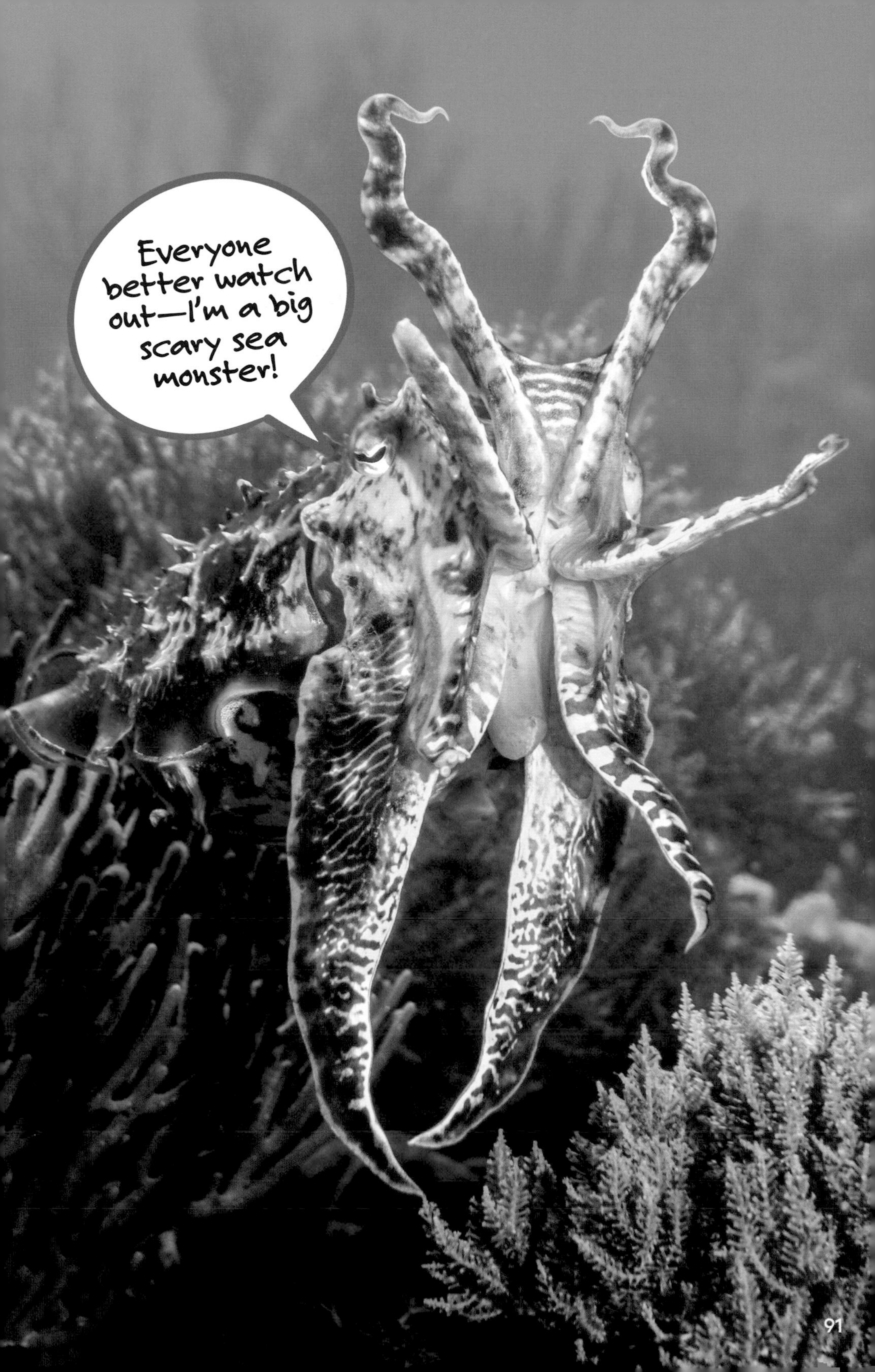
Everyone better watch out—I'm a big scary sea monster!

EMPEROR
PENGUINS

PENGUINS
ARE BIRDS THAT
CAN'T FLY
BUT CAN GRACEFULLY
SWIM
UNDERWATER.

INSIDER INFO

EMPEROR PENGUINS IN ANTARCTICA huddle together to stay warm in the freezing temperatures and winds. Hundreds or even thousands of them will pack together, taking turns standing on the coldest, outermost part of the circle in a process called social thermoregulation. By working together, all the penguins can stay warm and have a better chance of surviving.

PENGUIN

LOCATION: MARINE ENVIRONMENTS BELOW THE EQUATOR, IN ICY ANTARCTICA (5 SPECIES) AND SOME SPECIES IN TEMPERATE, WARMER CLIMATES

PRIMARY COMMUNICATION:

When baby penguins, called chicks, are looking for food, they'll make a peeping noise and bob their heads to get their parents' attention. Vocalizations and body language are just two ways that penguins communicate.

Penguins may not sing beautiful melodies like songbirds, but they do have a lot to say. Their grunts, chirps, and squeaks are loud and can travel more than half a mile (1 km) away. The pitch of these vocalizations, or sounds, helps penguins identify one another, just as humans identify one another by the tone of a person's voice. That's an important ability because penguins look almost identical. Using sound, mother penguins can find their babies, and partners can find each other in a sea of creatures that all look very similar.

Although these noises can be very loud and overwhelming to an outsider, they make sense to a penguin community. Penguins make many separate calls, each with a different meaning: that the animal is hungry, angry, scared, and happy, for example. African penguins make a donkey-like grunt when they are looking for a partner. Gentoo penguins in the Antarctic region make a buzzing noise when they are calling a group of penguins together to hunt for krill in the ocean. They understand that they are more likely to find food faster as a group.

Penguins also have body language that corresponds with these calls. During a "contact call," which is a penguin's way of saying hello, a penguin stands up and turns its half-open beak to the sky. During a "display call," when penguins are trying to get the attention of a family member, they stretch out their wings and open their beaks wide.

GENTOO PENGUIN

HUMPBACK WHALE

LOCATION: OCEANS

PRIMARY COMMUNICATION:

If another humpback whale comes near a mother and her calf (baby), the male will blow a cloud of bubbles from his blowhole. This acts as a screen to hide the mother and baby as they move underwater. They may do this when a boat approaches, too. In this way, male humpback whales provide protection and say, "Back off!" to any intruders.

They'll also protect their family with body language: An angry humpback may lash its fluke (the two fins of its tail) against the surface of the water, which creates a loud slapping noise above and below the water. Called lobtailing, this can also mean "Stay back."

After a whale finds its mate, the pair uses body language to communicate. They swim in a line, then roll and flip around, then dive below in tandem. Next, they stick their heads and flippers out of the water and then belly flop back into the ocean together. This parallel dance means "I like you." A whale will also grab the attention of its partner by lying on its back and slapping the water with its extra-long flippers.

During the winter, when male humpback whales are looking for a female partner, they make their famous call: a low and slow wailing noise. Scientists refer to these noises as songs because the tones change, and they can last 10 minutes or longer.

DR. WILD'S WORDS

HUMANS HAVE MADE THE OCEANS TOO LOUD. Activities such as recreational boating, shipping, and the digging done during energy exploration have filled the waters with ocean noise. Many marine animals cannot hear their prey, find their mate or their babies, or navigate. Species such as the blue whale are believed to be changing the pitch of their songs when they communicate. By blowing air more slowly, they lower their pitch, which scientists think may be their response to increased ocean noise.

Say What?

THERE ARE TWO KINDS OF WHALES: TOOTHED AND BALEEN. There are 65 species of toothed whales, including beluga whales, narwhals, orcas, and bottlenose dolphins. They have one blowhole, which is a nostril on top of their head. Baleen whales include 15 species—blue whales, gray whales, and humpback whales among them. A baleen whale is larger and has two blowholes on top of its head.

HUMPBACKS CAN **DIVE AS DEEP** AS **656 FEET (200 M)** AND STAY SUBMERGED FOR UP TO 20 MINUTES.

ONE **PUFFERFISH** CONTAINS ENOUGH **POISON** TO KILL 30 ADULT HUMANS.

PUFFERFISH (BLOWFISH)

LOCATION: OCEANS

PRIMARY
COMMUNICATION: 👁 👃

When a pufferfish senses it is in danger of being eaten, it can suck water into its stomach, which expands so that the fish grows to be as much as three times its original size. Pufferfish have very stretchy stomachs and can take in a lot of water very quickly. Puffing up sends a message to a predator: "Don't eat me." Of course, the spines on their skin help send out a warning sign, too.

In addition to these forms of visual communication, the pufferfish communicates using chemicals. If a pufferfish is eaten before it can inflate, it has a backup plan. It releases a bad-tasting, poisonous substance that can kill some fish. Talk about sending a message!

When male pufferfish want to attract a mate, they create beautiful circular patterns in the seafloor. They flap their fins as they swim around to create a seven-foot (2-m)-wide display of sand art with ridges and valleys. They even decorate the pattern with shell pieces. It can take a whole week to make. Females visit the detailed pattern and, if they like it, they'll partner with the male.

INSIDER INFO

SCIENTISTS USED TO BELIEVE THAT PUFFERFISH were holding their breath while they were inflated. Now they know that's not true. Pufferfish breathe normally through their gills while inflated. But when they deflate (like this one pictured), and are no longer in a defensive posture with spines out, they start breathing heavily. It can take up to five hours before their breathing returns to normal.

MALE MALLARD

DUCK

LOCATION: SHALLOW FRESHWATER PONDS, WETLANDS

PRIMARY COMMUNICATION:

Ducks squeak, whistle, coo, quack, and croak. And they learn how to do this when they are still unhatched ducklings. Two days before ducklings are born, they begin to vocalize, or make sounds. They are responding to their mother, who has been making calling noise as she sits on her eggs. The unhatched ducklings can hear their brothers and sisters chirping, too, and this helps them hatch around the same time.

Soon, they'll recognize their siblings and mother by the sound of their quacks. When ducklings hear their mother call to them from outside the nest, they'll follow her voice. They quack back and forth to keep the group together. This constant communication keeps the ducklings safe. All of these noises are considered calls, not songs. A call is short and instinctive, like the way we say "Ouch!" when we touch something hot.

Male and female ducks look different—the males are usually brighter in color and have curlier tail feathers. Males also share another trait: Their trachea and syrinx, which are parts of the throat, are shaped differently from those of females. That means females and males make very different sounds. For example, female wood ducks make a loud, high-pitched squeal when they are scared. But male wood ducks can't make that sound. Male mallards can make a grunt-whistle to attract female ducks. But female mallards can't make that call in return.

Ducks also use body language. When a male wants to impress a female, he makes grunting and whistling noises, and his head, wings, and tail turn upward. Males and females will bob their heads up and down, sometimes splashing the water, if they like each other.

DUCKS HAVE **ACCENTS.** CITY DUCKS HAVE A SHOUTING QUACK WHILE COUNTRY DUCKS HAVE A SOFTER VOICE.

C'mon ducklings, let's move it!

SEAHORSE

LOCATION: OCEANS

PRIMARY COMMUNICATION: 👁 👂

Seahorses make clicking noises when they want to show that they like each other. They're also known to make a deep growling noise when they are caught by a predator or are in some other kind of distress. It's a way of saying, "Don't touch me." The sound is so low that it can't be heard by humans but it causes their bodies to vibrate. This can startle a predator, giving the seahorse a chance to escape.

A seahorse also communicates through body language and visual cues that involve changing the color of its body like a chameleon (pp. 48–49). When it wants to find a mate, it performs a special dance. The male seahorse changes colors while circling around the female and clicking quietly. She'll click back if she likes him. The clicks are so quiet that predators such as sea turtles and crabs can't hear them. Next, the couple twists their tails together and then floats away. They perform this dance each morning as a way to renew their bond, as if to say, "Let's stick together." Once they've picked a mate, seahorses stay partners for life.

INSIDER INFO

BECAUSE THEY AREN'T great swimmers, seahorses wait for food like plankton and algae to drift in the ocean currents toward them. They suck up the food with their snouts like a vacuum. Seahorses have to eat 30 to 50 times a day. That's because they don't have a stomach to store food. Their meal moves through their body very quickly, so they get hungry more frequently.

SEAHORSES **"HITCHHIKE"** BY GRABBING ON TO A PIECE OF FLOATING **SEAWEED** OR ANCHOR IN PLACE BY **WRAPPING THEIR TAIL** AROUND **SEAGRASS** OR **CORAL.**

A male (orange) circles his partner (yellow).

Wow, I can't believe what that mockingbird just said.

DURING A STORM, THE **SKELETON** OF A **MARINE IGUANA** **SHRINKS** UP TO 20 PERCENT. IT **GROWS** BACK TO SIZE ONCE THE WEATHER CLEARS.

MARINE IGUANA

LOCATION: ROCKY SHORELINE OF THE GALÁPAGOS ISLANDS

PRIMARY COMMUNICATION:

The marine iguana is the only ocean-swimming lizard in the world, and in 2007, scientists found that it's the only nonvocal animal to respond to another animal's communication cues. Although the marine iguana can't make sounds, it eavesdrops, or listens in, on the songs and alarm calls of the Galápagos mockingbird. The alarm calls tell them a predator, like a hawk, is nearby. When they hear this call, they react quickly and try to escape. This is called heterospecific communication, which means information transfer between different species. Marine iguanas are preyed upon by Galápagos hawks an average of two times per day. Because the rocky shoreline makes it hard for marine iguanas to see much above themselves, without the alarm call of the mockingbird they might not know a hawk is near until it is too late.

Male marine iguanas use color to attract females. Some turn from black to bright red during the mating season. Others turn a mix of red and green, which earned them the nickname "Christmas iguanas."

Once they've attracted a group of females, they guard them against other males. They use body language to protect the females, bobbing their heads to warn other males to stay away. If another male approaches, they will butt their heads together and push each other backward. Whichever iguana loses the fight has to leave.

Say What? MARINE IGUANAS like to pile on top of one another, sometimes forming a pile of as many as 200. Usually reptiles like to be alone. But after taking long dives (up to one hour) in the cold waters of the Galápagos Islands, where they eat algae from underwater rocks, these iguanas climb on top of one another to get warm.

DOLPHIN DIALOGUE

In the 1970s, researcher Dr. Louis Herman proved that dolphins could understand hundreds of commands. He did this by creating a sign language and teaching two bottlenose dolphins, Phoenix and Akeakamai, how to respond to those gestures. But this is just one-way communication, meaning the human talking to the dolphin. A command is made, the dolphin understands, and it performs an action in response. It's similar to how a dolphin trainer might teach a dolphin to do tricks.

Scientists continued to study dolphin communication. They learned that dolphins were naturally able to associate a sound with an object and were also able to mimic sounds. For example, each dolphin has a signature whistle that acts like a name. When a dolphin wants to get another dolphin's attention, it can mimic its signature whistle. This discovery gave scientists further hope that one day we could "talk" to these marine mammals.

Today, Dr. Denise Herzing is a leader in dolphin communication. For more than 30 years, she's been studying wild dolphins in the Bahamas. Her first goal was to bond with the wild dolphins. Then she developed an underwater keyboard that dolphins could touch with their snouts. Each of the four keys represented a different toy, such as a ball, and soon the dolphins learned how to use it. Finally, dolphins were "talking" to humans. But now it was the humans who couldn't talk back.

Today, Herzing and her team of researchers use an underwater device called CHAT (Cetacean Hearing and Telemetry). It can send out artificial whistle sounds that Herzog hopes the wild dolphins will learn and mimic. She will associate the whistles with an object, such as seaweed. It's kind of like the people and the dolphins are creating a new language together. Eventually, this language would allow humans and dolphins to communicate back and forth with each other. So far, the dolphins have mimicked the whistles and then added on their own whistle afterward. Dr. Herzing is still researching what this could mean. While it is incredible progress, translating any animal's communication will take a very long time.

DR. HERMAN SIGNALS TO A DOLPHIN.

DR. HERZING (RIGHT) AND HER TEAM PREPARE TO USE CHAT.

4

IN THE AIR

STEP OUTSIDE AND LISTEN. Do you hear sounds whirring above and around you? Birds and insects are always communicating with each other both day and night. Some of these sounds, such as those of a bat, are beyond the hearing range of humans. Others, like the notes of a sweet songbird, sound like music to our ears. Some airborne animals also know how to put on a sky-high show. These visual displays all send very different messages. Let's see what the birds, bats, and bees have to say.

TUFTED
TITMOUSE

BLUE AND GOLD
MACAW

OF ALL **350** PARROT SPECIES, **AFRICAN** GRAY PARROTS ARE THE BEST MIMICS.

DR. WILD'S WORDS

SOME OF MY FAVORITE PATIENTS have been parrots because I can use human words to communicate with them directly, and they can respond in the same language I use. For example, when I want to examine a parrot, I hold my finger out and tell them, "Step up." When I work with some really well-trained birds, I can get them to open their wings or open their mouth for a treat. Some of these birds have learned what these words actually mean.

PARROT

LOCATION: TROPICAL FORESTS

PRIMARY COMMUNICATION:

When a parrot wants to get the attention of another bird, it bows and bobs its head. It also uses its feathers to send messages. When a parrot's back feathers are fluffed and its tail feathers are fanned, it's expressing anger. When it flips its wings up and down (but not to fly), it's trying to get attention or express frustration.

This body language is important because parrots—a group that includes macaws, lovebirds, and cockatoos—are very social birds. They live in flocks, usually with 20 to 30 other birds, so squawks, screams, and screeches are necessary to help keep their flock together.

Known for their curved beaks, bright colors, and songs, some species of parrots stand out for something else: mimicking. This means they can imitate a sound they hear. In the wild, parrots will mimic the calls of other birds and mammals around them. Scientists believe mimicking one another's noises helps the birds create a bond and makes them feel that they belong. This is why they mimic human sounds, too, like words and phrases. They want to fit in. But just because they say a word doesn't mean that they understand it. In fact, they'll mimic just about anything—including the ding of a microwave timer or the ringtone of a cell phone.

Say What? SCIENTISTS BELIEVE that all animals are born knowing how to speak the entirety of their species' "language." They don't learn to speak it, word by word, or sound by sound, like humans do. But parrots, songbirds, hummingbirds, and others can learn how to make new sounds. For example, nightingales have the ability to learn so many new sounds that they can sing as many as 60 different songs with their expanded "vocabulary."

Want to hear my new song?

NIGHTINGALE

BAT

LOCATION: CAVES, TREES

PRIMARY COMMUNICATION: 👂 👃 👁

When a male bat wants to impress a female, he will spread his wings, sing, and the long hairs on the top of his head stand up. The singing noise that bats make is like that of a songbird's, with trills and up and down notes. Each male sings a unique tune. This noise is often too high for humans to hear. Bats also use singing to identify each other, scare off predators, and teach their offspring. Scientists believe bats may use vocalizations because sound can travel far. By vocalizing, a bat can stay in one place and send a message across a distance instead of using its energy to fly there.

After studying 22 Egyptian fruit bats for 75 days, scientists discovered that the bats weren't just squeaking—they were arguing. They were fighting about food and sleeping space. And sometimes the squeak meant "Get away!" These squeaks were directed toward a specific bat, which means the bats were having one-on-one conversations.

Bats use chemical communication, too. With scent glands on their neck and chin, bats can mark their territory by rubbing their chin against a surface near their home. This helps bats define their status and claim a prime location at the top of a tree or cave instead of one of the lower edges. It's their way of saying, "This is MY spot."

DR. WILD'S WORDS

AFTER HUMANS, BATS ARE THE MOST VOCAL MAMMALS. That's because they "see" by "talking." This is called echolocation. Bats' high-pitched noises bounce off objects around them and return as an echo. Bats can tell the difference between the echo from a tree, a human, a mosquito, or another bat. Because they rely on echolocation, bats become temporarily "blind" while they eat. They can't make a noise with a mouth full of food.

THE WORLD'S **SMALLEST MAMMAL** IS THE **BUMBLEBEE BAT**. IT WEIGHS **LESS THAN** A PENNY.

Oh, hi there!

LUCAS'S SHORT-NOSED FRUIT BAT

HONEYBEE

LOCATION: MEADOWS, WOODLANDS

PRIMARY COMMUNICATION: 👁 👃

Honeybees can "speak" through a dance language. There are many honeybee dances, including the "round dance," "sickle dance," and "waggle dance," which is the most studied. When a worker bee returns to the nest and starts "dancing" up and down within her hive, her sisters and half sisters stay near her and actually try to touch her. They are trying to calculate the location of the new food source she has found. Scientists also believe the scout bees carry the scent of the flower with them, which helps the other bees locate it.

Bees also use smell to locate and protect their hives. If the bees in the hive don't recognize the scent of a bee that comes near the hive, the bees inside will make sure it doesn't enter. When a bee stings a human or animal, it releases chemicals called pheromones that send a danger signal to other bees, as if to say: "I'm threatened," or "Stay away," or "Help me!" (This scent remains on your clothes and could later attract bees that are ready to fight. That's why you should wash your clothes after getting stung.)

Hives are filled by tens of thousands of bees but are run by only one: the queen bee. She can guide the behavior of all the other bees with pheromones. These chemicals say a lot. They tell the female worker bees to keep working. They also tell the male drone bees to be her mate. And they tell the colony, "Your queen is alive and well."

HONEYBEES ARE POLLINATORS, which means they move pollen from flower to flower. Pollination helps plants produce fruit and seeds. More than 1,000 plants that we rely on for food, drinks, and medicine must be pollinated. But bees and other pollinating animals are threatened. One way to help honeybees is to plant nectar-rich native flowers at home or in your neighborhood.

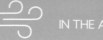
FLAMINGO

LOCATION: LAGOONS, SHALLOW LAKES

PRIMARY COMMUNICATION:

Flamingos are noisy! These bright pink birds honk, grunt, and growl to keep their flock together. The noises also help mother and father flamingos recognize their chicks, or babies.

With those long legs and long necks, it's no surprise that flamingos use posturing, a type of body language, to communicate, too. And it's not just one flamingo that makes a move to send a message—usually the whole flock moves together. These displays remind the flamingos to mate. For example, stretching their S-shaped necks while pointing their hooked bills to the sky is called "head-flagging." The "wing salute" involves spreading the wings while the neck is outstretched. Flamingos even march in time together in quick steps and will change directions without missing a beat.

Flamingos also use a posture to send an alarm call. When an eagle, hyena, or other predator is nearby, one flamingo will stretch out its neck until it's in a straight, vertical position. Soon, the rest of the flock copies that movement. This posture signals that it's time for all the birds to take flight because there is immediate danger.

Living in a flock keeps the flamingos safe. With more birds as lookouts—and able to share warnings quickly—they are all more likely to survive.

 **DR. WILD'S WORDS**

FLAMINGOS ARE what they eat. Flamingos are born with gray or white feathers, but they eventually turn pink because of their diet. There's a natural pinkish dye found in the shrimp and blue-green algae that they eat. The more flamingos eat, the deeper the shade of pink, red, or orange they become—including their beaks. If they don't eat enough, they will fade back to white.

FLAMINGOS CAN **GROW** TO BE **FOUR** TO **FIVE** FEET (1.2 TO 1.5 M) TALL BUT ONLY **WEIGH** BETWEEN **FOUR** AND **EIGHT** POUNDS (1.8 TO 3.6 KG).

Wheeeee!

FLYING SQUIRRELS CAN **GLIDE** FOR ALMOST **300 FEET** (91 M). THAT'S NEARLY THE LENGTH OF A **SOCCER FIELD.**

FLYING SQUIRREL

LOCATION: FORESTS, WOODLANDS

PRIMARY COMMUNICATION: 👁 👂 👃

Young flying squirrels make high-pitched squeaks—tseets—when they are worried or suffering. This is just one of the many birdlike noises that flying squirrels use to communicate. When they are angry or scared, they cluck. They're also known to make soft chirping sounds. As they chase another flying squirrel in order to find a mate, they make squealing noises and churrs.

Flying squirrels have a thin layer of skin, almost like a parachute, between their front and back limbs that they can stretch out and that allows them to catch the wind. While they are not actually flying, they do glide from tree to tree. So not only do they sound like birds, but they also soar like them.

If you shine an ultraviolet light at a North American flying squirrel, it will glow a fluorescent pink color. What does that mean? Scientists aren't positive, but they have noticed that these flying squirrels glow more brightly on their undersides. Some scientists believe that this could be a way they communicate with other flying squirrels or predators. Or it could help them navigate over snowy areas.

Female flying squirrels use body language when they feel threatened. They'll lunge forward and stomp their front feet. They may even slap the faces of their opponent. Ouch!

INSIDER INFO

NOT MANY PEOPLE KNOW that flying squirrels are commonly found in North America. Some have even adapted to live in cities and suburbs where there are enough tall trees. So why don't we see them as often as we see the eastern gray squirrel, which seems to always be running through parks and backyards? Because flying squirrels are nocturnal, which means they only come out at night, when humans are often asleep or indoors.

BUTTERFLY

LOCATION: GRASSLANDS, WOODLANDS, FARMLANDS

PRIMARY COMMUNICATION:

MEADOW BROWN BUTTERFLY

Male butterflies can create noises with their wings. These noises serve two purposes: to attract females and to tell other males to stay away. When a male finds a female he likes during the night, he will fly around her in a circle. This helps him waft his scent all around her. Some of these scents can be picked up by butterflies that are 10 miles (16 km) away. The scent is a type of pheromone. Pheromones help butterflies communicate at night, when their colored wings can't be seen.

Butterflies also use their brightly colored wings to communicate with one another. Different colors and patterns allow them to recognize their own species. They are also a way for them to tell which is male or female and to help them find a mate.

A butterfly's bold and bright wings are also a way of saying, "Don't eat me! I'm poisonous," to predators like birds. Even if they are not poisonous, their bright colors act as a warning symbol. Big "eyes" or spots that appear on some wings are another way they stay safe. These make a butterfly or moth look much bigger than the tiny insect it really is.

LARGE SKIPPER

THE **FASTEST BUTTERFLIES,** CALLED **SKIPPERS,** CAN FLY AS FAST AS **37 MILES AN HOUR** (60 KM/H).

TAU EMPEROR MOTH

INSIDER INFO

BUTTERFLIES AND MOTHS are part of the same family. So how can you tell them apart? Moths' wings lie flat, their bodies are larger and furrier, and they usually fly at night. Butterflies tend to rest with their wings up, have longer and smoother antennae, and usually fly during the day.

OWL

LOCATION: MANY HABITATS WORLDWIDE, FROM FORESTS TO DESERTS

PRIMARY COMMUNICATION:

Everyone knows that an owl hoots, but did you also know that it whistles, barks, and yelps, too? It turns out that owls make a lot of sounds. The barn owl makes a screechlike *kr-r-r-ick*. The eastern screech owl sounds something like a horse's whinny. The nighttime hooting noise you'd probably recognize the most—a true *hoot-hoot-hoot*—is from the great horned owl. But what do these noises mean?

Among barn owls, a screech occurs when a male and female are chasing each other as they fly through the air. It means they may want to be each other's mate. But a repeated scream means an owl is in pain or is scared. When defending itself against a predator, such as an eagle or a snake, an owl will hiss and then loudly yell. If there's an intruder in an owl's tree—an animal the owl simply doesn't like—the owl will spread its wings, sway its head back and forth, and snap its beak. If the animal doesn't leave, the owl will fall backward and strike the intruder with its feet, which are equipped with sharp talons.

BURROWING OWLS

DR. WILD'S WORDS

OWLS HAVE VERY flexible necks. They can twist their heads 270 degrees, which is almost one complete circle. They do this because their eyeballs can't move; they are locked in place. Whereas humans can simply shift their eyeballs from side to side without moving their heads, owls have to turn their heads if they want to see anything beside them.

AN **OWL** CAN HEAR A **MOUSE MAKING NOISE** FROM 75 FEET (23 M) AWAY.

RAVENS CAN **FLY UPSIDE DOWN** AND DO **SOMERSAULTS** IN MIDAIR.

RAVEN

LOCATION: FORESTS

PRIMARY COMMUNICATION:

Ravens use nonverbal signals to communicate, such as pointing with their beaks. They also pick up moss, twigs, and other objects with their beak and "present" them to other birds. It's the raven's way of saying, "Look at this." The other bird then will stop, look, and might pick up the object, too. Ravens were the first animal identified outside of a primate species to do this. They are considered very intelligent creatures and have been known to hide food from other ravens and work together to come up with sneaky ways to steal food from animals and humans. This might involve playing dead, pulling fishing lines out of the water, or causing a distraction.

Ravens can also communicate by making calls. They have more than 30 different categories of calls, including alarm, comfort, and defense. Their deep croak is the most common, and scientists have observed them making this call as a response to the sounds of nearby ravens. If a predator is close, they'll repeat a short shrill call over and over. When ravens pair up with a mate, they learn each other's calls. That way one raven can get the other raven's attention if it's gone missing. When males sing to defend their territory, the females will join in. The singing becomes an alternating duet. This allows the ravens to protect their land and stay near each other, especially in a dense forest where it can be hard to keep an eye on each other.

INSIDER INFO

CROWS AND RAVENS look a lot alike. The next time you see a black bird flying above, knowing these differences can help you identify which is which: Ravens are larger and travel in twos. Crows travel in groups. Ravens make low croaks or screams, while crows make a traditional *caw* noise. Ravens tend to soar through the air, while crows tend to flap their wings more often. Ravens are more common on the West Coast of the United States and are seen less often on the East Coast.

LADYBUG

LOCATION: GRASSLANDS, MEADOWS, FORESTS, WETLANDS, URBAN AREAS

PRIMARY COMMUNICATION: 🔔 👁

Ladybugs know how to play dead to protect themselves. Because many predators prefer to eat live prey, ladybugs flop on their back and pretend they are not alive. This move can keep danger away. Ladybugs' bright coloring also protects them. They can be yellow, orange, or red, but they are most known for the polka-dotted shell that protects their wings. These bright colors tell their predators, "Stay away!"

If a predator does attack, ladybugs release a stinky smelling and bad-tasting yellow fluid from their knee area. That chemical can be toxic to some predators such as birds and small mammals. Soon predators associate the bad smell and taste with the bright color.

Ladybugs gather in groups of hundreds or thousands in order to diapause, which is the insect term for hibernation. Some scientists believe they gather in such big numbers to stay warm—when many gather close together their body temperatures rise. In order for all of these hundreds or thousands of ladybugs to find one another, they release chemical cues. These scents help them diapause in a safe place together.

It's time for diapause!

ZZZZZ...

THE
MOST SPOTS A
LADYBUG
CAN HAVE IS
24.

VIOLET-TAILED SYLPH
HUMMINGBIRD

THE TINY
RUBY-THROATED
HUMMINGBIRD
IS JUST **THREE INCHES**
TO **3.5 INCHES** (7.5 TO
9 CM) LONG.

RUBY-THROATED
HUMMINGBIRD

HUMMINGBIRD

LOCATION: RAINFORESTS, WOODLANDS, DESERTS

PRIMARY COMMUNICATION:

Tiny hummingbirds move incredibly quickly, and their call is fast, too. This quick squeaking call is a threat that means "Back off!" If any other bird flies into its territory, the hummingbird will make this squeak: a single note repeated over and over again. The note gets louder with each squeak. And if the invader doesn't fly away, it will be chased out. A hummingbird may dive at other birds or strike them midair with its long beak.

These tiny birds are also known for their bold colors, which are mostly blue and green. Their brilliant colors are another way that the birds communicate with one another. Hummingbirds are solitary creatures except in the spring, when it's time to find a mate. Bright and shiny feathers on a male tell the female that he is healthy. He'll flash his feathers to catch a female's attention. If she seems interested, he'll perform a special dance with looping dives as a way to convince her to choose him as her partner.

INSIDER INFO

EVEN THOUGH THEY HAVE FEWER FEATHERS than any other species of bird, hummingbirds are impressive fliers. They can soar backward, sideways, and upside down. And they can easily hover in place. That means they can attack by surprise and outfly just about any other bird. It's a good thing they are such capable fliers—their legs are too short for them to walk or hop well.

Check it out—I'm flying backward!

RUBY-TOPAZ HUMMINGBIRDS

LYREBIRD

LOCATION: FORESTS

PRIMARY COMMUNICATION:

Lyrebirds can mimic, or copy, the sound of almost anything they hear, from other bird species to human-made sounds like a camera, car alarm, or even a chain saw! Male superb lyrebirds attract mates by singing songs that piece together these copycat sounds with noises of their own—like twanging, whirring, and whistling. About 80 percent of the song is mimicked noises. The male sings this song for about 20 minutes from a display mound, a small pile of dirt that he has built. The louder and more complex the song, the more impressed a female will be.

After the song draws a female nearer, the male uses body language for one final display. He raises his long tailfeathers over his head and shakes them in a dance-like movement. He may also jump, bob, and step to the side. Scientists have observed that certain songs are always matched with certain movements. This means male lyrebirds have created choreography, or a memorized series of steps.

Female lyrebirds are vocal, too, and can mimic other bird species as well. They can also sing 20 different alarm calls, including a loud shrieking noise. But scientists believe their singing is mostly used to protect their offspring. Their whistles and cackling calls may serve to keep predators away from their territory.

Say What? EVEN THOUGH LYREBIRDS are included in this chapter with other birds, they don't really fly. Their muscles are weak, so their wings are used mainly for hopping onto branches or rocks, and then gliding back down to the forest floor. And even though they're known to roost in trees, they mostly live on the ground, which makes them terrestrial birds (birds that cannot or do not often fly), the same as quails, pheasants, turkeys, ostriches, and roadrunners.

WHEN A MALE **LYREBIRD** SPREADS HIS **TAILFEATHERS** THEY LOOK LIKE A **LYRE (A HARP-LIKE INSTRUMENT** FROM ANCIENT GREECE).

CLICK That was my camera sound! Pretty good, right?

DR. WILD'S WORDS

BIRDS HAVE USED THEIR SINGING TO FORM COLONIES, to flock or fly together, to forage, and more. Some of their most elaborate displays of song and dance are used when they are trying to mate. Most songbirds do not learn just one song. In fact, the song sparrow sings 10 different songs, the western marsh wren sings more than a hundred songs, and the brown thrasher sings a thousand different songs!

MOSQUITO

LOCATION: FORESTS, MARSHES

PRIMARY COMMUNICATION:

Even though mosquitoes are solitary, which means they like to be alone, they still need to communicate with one another. The vibrating sound made by their wings as they fly can help them find another mosquito. The female's wings make a lower- pitched noise, and the flapping of the male wings makes a higher-pitched noise. When a male and female mosquito are flying near each other and if they sync up their wing flapping to the exact same speed and tone, it means they are willing to mate with each other.

Female mosquitoes, however, are more interested in finding creatures other than mosquitoes because they need to eat their blood. (Male mosquitoes drink nectar from flowers.) Some species bite only certain animals like amphibians or birds, but others will bite whatever they can find—including humans. A mosquito can sense the carbon dioxide in an animal's breath from more than 30 feet (9.1 m) away. Then it will smell the chemicals in its sweat with its antennae. Finally, it detects the heat coming from an animal's skin. Its legs can "taste" the skin and find the perfect spot to bite. Receiving these signals from another animal—and then taking action—is a form of communication.

SPEAK UP

STUDYING HOW MOSQUITOES communicate with each other and the world around them can help save lives. That's because mosquitoes can carry diseases, like malaria, that make humans sick. If we better understand how mosquitoes mate and why they bite humans, scientists can come up with better ways to help reduce malaria. You can help by raising funds and awareness for groups that work to help stop the spread of this deadly disease.

Learning how to cover a bed with a mosquito net can save lives.

MOSQUITOES BEAT THEIR WINGS **300** TO **600** TIMES EVERY SECOND.

SONGBIRD

LOCATION: GRASSLANDS, FORESTS

PRIMARY COMMUNICATION: 🦻 👁

One songbird species, called the Japanese great tit, uses syntax when it communicates. This means that each sound it makes has a meaning and that when it strings those sounds together in certain ways it creates different meanings. It's the same as how humans string words together to create different sentences. This is the only animal, besides humans, known to do this.

About half of the world's birds are songbirds. These birds sing pretty tunes, of course, but the strings of notes you hear repeated over and over again also have a purpose. Males are usually the ones who belt out the long, multinote songs. They sing for two reasons: to let females know they are looking for a mate and to defend their territory. It's a way to tell other males, "Stay away!"

These long, loud songs travel far because songbirds have a syrinx, or vocal organ, near their lungs. This is different from a human's vocal cords, which are located near the top of our throat. Birds can sing for minutes at a time without having to catch their breath. The kakapo can be heard from four miles (6.4 km) away. Scientists believe birds may sing at dawn because there is less wind, noise, and other sounds to interfere with delivery of their message. That means their songs can be heard more easily.

Birds also make call notes, which are shorter and simpler than songs. Each of these notes means something different. Calls can be peeps and chirps in smaller birds or caws and screeches in larger birds. For example, a specific note might mean that a predator is on the ground nearby. Or it may be a call to another bird to ensure they stay near each other in flight.

Say What? SONGBIRDS INCLUDE WRENS, larks, swallows, sparrows, warblers, and more. Each of these species has a distinct call. Some birders (people who study birds as a hobby) can identify a bird just by hearing its song. They listen to the number of notes and whether the tune rises or falls. Some even translate bird calls to English words or sounds to help them identify a bird song. For example, the common yellowthroat sounds like it's singing *witchity-witchity-witchity.*

COMMON YELLOWTHROAT

BOWERBIRD

LOCATION: RAINFORESTS

PRIMARY COMMUNICATION:

Male bowerbirds build impressive structures, called bowers, on the ground using twigs. They decorate the bowers with colorful flowers, stones, leaves, snail shells, and bones. Some bowerbirds even "paint" the walls with plant juices and use bark or their beak as a brush. Bowers can be many shapes, from domed tunnels of sticks to maypole-like tents with colorful "front yards" that may take two months to build. Building this structure is one way that male bowerbirds use visual displays to attract females. It's their way of saying, "Look how talented I am!" If a female likes a bower, she will approach the male.

Male bowerbirds also attract nearby females by making the dark pupils of their yellow eyes grow and then shrink. The female responds, acknowledging this mesmerizing display, by making a wheezing-like call. Finally, the female will outstretch one wing slowly and then shake it rapidly. If the female likes what she sees, she'll pick up a piece of fruit in her beak and throw it to the male. Then he'll butt her chest with his head a few times.

Bowerbirds make many vocalizations, too. They chatter, hiss, and cackle. A female makes these sounds if her nest is disturbed. Bowerbirds can also mimic the calls of other bird species.

She's gonna love what I did with the place...

BOWERBIRDS **STEAL** FROM ONE ANOTHER. AN ESPECIALLY COLORFUL **DECORATION** MAY GET PLUCKED FROM ONE BIRD'S **BOWER** AND END UP IN ANOTHER'S.

EAGLE

LOCATION: TUNDRA, FORESTS

PRIMARY COMMUNICATION: 👁 👂

Eagles have a handful of different calls they use to communicate with each other. Golden eagles repeat a high-pitched noise over and over again when they are trying to attract a mate. They are also known to chirp, honk, hiss, and cluck. They call to their nestlings (babies), and their nestlings call back when they are hungry. Bald eagles chirp and whistle, but they also make a unique sound called a peal, which is a long, high-pitched cry they make when they feel threatened.

Although eagles use vocalizations to communicate, they are mostly quiet birds. That's where another form of communication comes in.

Eagles use body language to express their wants and needs. Male golden eagles perform complicated flight patterns in the sky high above when they want to defend their territory below—and protect their chicks. If a bird enters their space, they'll raise the feathers on their heads, stretch their neck forward, and open their wings.

Male golden eagles also put on shows to impress females. They fly high in the air, fold their wings, and then drop headfirst. They plummet toward the ground, then spread their wings and begin soaring again. Bald eagles perform similarly, but males and females do it together. They lock on to each other's talons and tumble and twist toward the ground. They let go before they hit.

Say What? BALD EAGLES aren't actually bald. Their heads are covered with short, white feathers. They appear on American coins and stamps and are used as a symbol of freedom. When the Founding Fathers of the United States discussed choosing the eagle as a symbol for the country, Benjamin Franklin disagreed. He thought bald eagles were lazy because they steal food from other birds.

EAGLES CAN MOVE THEIR HEADS ABOUT 270 DEGREES—JUST LIKE AN OWL.

BALD EAGLE

FOR THE BIRDS

One of the most famous birds to ever live was Alex the African gray parrot. His owner, Dr. Irene Pepperberg, taught him more than 150 English words. When shown a blue paper triangle, he could name the color, the shape, and what it was made out of. He could also count up the total number of objects placed before him as well as add two small numbers together. This took a lot of training.

Scientists compared his language skills to those of primates like Koko the gorilla. But some scientists argue that Alex wasn't really communicating—he was simply performing a trick. Birds like parrots are imitating, or mimicking, human

DR. PEPPERBERG PLAYS WITH ALEX.

language. They are "vocal learners" because they can hear a sound and then try to make that sound themselves.

Alex's final words to Dr. Pepperberg were "I love you." But scientists don't know if Alex knew what "love" meant. Just because a parrot can make sounds that resemble words, it doesn't mean that the parrot understands those words. For example, even though some parrots can memorize words, they can't string the words they've memorized together to form a new sentence. But they may understand the context, or the correct timing, of when to use the words. For example, "goodbye" is said at the end of the day.

Many animal species that seem to communicate with humans are social animals, which means they like and need to be around others. Mimicking speech could be one way they bond with humans, the same way that some birds mimic another bird's song. Parrots are known to want to fit in with their flock. And if you take a parrot out of the wild and put it with a group of humans, it will try to fit in with the "flock" of humans, too.

CHAPTER

5

BY OUR SIDE

I N THIS SECTION, we'll look at the animals we find living among us as well as those animals that we've invited to our homes and farms. Domesticated animals, or animals that have been adapted for human use, are companion animals like pets or farm animals like cows. These animals often spend time bonding with humans, but they still have a language all their own. So let's listen to gerbils chirp and purr, find the reason horses smile, and try to figure out why Fido keeps barking. While the animals in this chapter are often found in homes and on farms, in the "location" section, we've listed where they are found in the wild.

POMERANIAN

142

DOG

LOCATION: TUNDRA, FORESTS, PRAIRIES

PRIMARY COMMUNICATION: 🔔 👂 👁

D ogs howl, bark, snarl, growl, yip, yap, and—of course—woof. While they obviously use verbal communication, they are excellent nonverbal communicators, too. Their body language—from their tail to their ears to their eyes to their facial expression—says a lot about what they are likely thinking and feeling.

A dog with a wagging tail, relaxed ears, and a slightly open mouth is probably content. If a dog wants to play, the front end of its body is lowered while its rear end remains up. You'll know a dog is fearful when it's trembling, its tail is tucked, and its ears are flattened. Hair raised, nose wrinkled, and teeth bared means a dog is getting ready to attack. It's a dog's way of saying, "Watch out. I'll bite if I have to."

Dogs also communicate through smell; it's actually their main form of communication. Their sense of smell is a thousand times stronger than a human's. There's a reason dogs sniff each other when they first meet. From one whiff they can learn if the dog is male or female, its mood, what it ate recently, and whomever else the dog met that day. Dogs can remember this information and recognize another dog they haven't seen in years. The scent of dog urine includes a lot of information, too. When dogs sniff a tree, they are sniffing pee left by other dogs and learning all about them.

SPEAK **UP**

EVERY YEAR, more than six million pets are taken to animal shelters. Half of those pets are dogs that need homes. You can help out the animal community by adopting your next pet from a shelter, or by offering a temporary foster home to a pet while an animal shelter or animal rescue finds it a forever home. Shelters and rescues are always looking for donations, too, including pet food, towels, blankets, and more.

PIG

LOCATION: SAVANNAS, FORESTS, SHRUBLANDS

PRIMARY COMMUNICATION:

Pigs live in family groups and are very social. They often communicate through sounds—and not just "oink." Scientists have identified 20 different vocalizations, including barks and screams.

Friendly grunts are a way of saying, "Hello." A deep grunt followed by a series of grunts is a way that mothers call to their piglets when it's time to eat. Pigs growl when they are mad and squeal when they are excited.

A loud roar, a short grunt, and a long growl are three different types of warning calls that mean "Danger."

Why so loud? Their ears pick up loud sounds better than they do quieter sounds. Together, these noises can help keep them safe.

Body postures can also be telling. As with other animals, a pig's ear and tail movements tell you how it is feeling. When pigs greet each other, they touch snouts. That's because they have scent glands all over their face. Through smell they can identify other pigs, navigate their way around, and find food.

DR. WILD'S WORDS

DESPITE THE POPULARITY OF THE PHRASE "sweating like a pig," pigs can't sweat. Pigs have only a few sweat glands, while humans have two to four million. Sweating helps humans cool down. When pigs need to cool down, they roll around in the mud. The mud acts like a sunblock and helps lower their body temperature by 3.6 degrees Fahrenheit (2 degrees Celsius). That's because the water in mud evaporates more slowly than water on its own, keeping the pig cooler for a longer time.

Aah ... this mud hits the spot.

PIGS ARE VERY **CLEAN.** THEY **PEE** AND **POO** IN A SEPARATE AREA, **FAR AWAY** FROM WHERE THEY **SLEEP** AND **EAT.**

HUMANS USUALLY CAN'T HEAR THE **SOFT PURR** OF A **GERBIL,** BUT WE CAN **FEEL** ITS LITTLE BODY **VIBRATE.**

GERBIL

LOCATION: DESERTS, GRASSLANDS, MOUNTAIN VALLEYS

PRIMARY COMMUNICATION: 👁️ 👂 👃 ✋

Gerbils are known to wink, which can mean a few different things, including "Thank you" or "Hello." Gerbils are social creatures, so they prefer to be around other gerbils, and they make gestures to show affection. For example, mother gerbils will groom their babies (pups) as a way to bond and communicate. Other gestures are bolder. When a male is attracted to a female, he stomps his feet while chasing her, which creates a thumping *da-dum da-dum* noise.

Gerbils will also touch noses and "kiss" when they meet. This greeting is another tactile, or physical, form of communication, and also a form of chemical communication. It allows gerbils to exchange information through the chemicals in their spit, or saliva. Their saliva reveals whether the gerbil is male or female as well as whether it is more dominant (a leader) or submissive (a follower).

A mother gerbil will also mark her pups with a scent by rubbing her stomach on top of the pups. Her stomach has a small scent gland, and when it emits the chemical smell, it means something like "Mine."

Pups chirp a lot. This could mean they are hungry or cold. Adult gerbils may squeak back and forth at each other to show affection, as if they are saying, "I like you." Gerbils also purr when they are happy. A very loud squeak could mean the gerbil is in pain or danger.

DR. WILD'S WORDS

GERBILS EAT THEIR own poop. Many young rodents do this. It's a way for them to get more vitamins. Vitamin B12 is an important vitamin that gerbils produce when their food is being digested. The only way young rodents can get this vitamin is by eating their vitamin-filled poop.

... What? It's healthy for us!

TURKEY

LOCATION: FORESTS, PASTURES, FIELDS

PRIMARY COMMUNICATION:

Turkeys are known for their "gobble," but did you know that hens (female turkeys) can't make that signature sound? They make a clucking noise instead, which is used to get the attention of another hen or a tom (male turkey). Turkeys can make about 15 different vocalizations in the wild. A loud series of yelps is an "assembly call" for when a hen wants to gather her flock together. When turkeys are content—when they are being fed, for instance—they make a soft purring sound.

Male turkeys use the sound of *gobble, gobble* to keep other males away and to attract the attention of a female. They combine this vocal communication with an impressive display of body language: a dance called tidbitting, in which the turkey bobs its head while its red wattle, a fleshy piece of skin that hangs from its chin, flops around. Male turkeys will also strut, fan out their tail feathers, throw their head back, and walk with their wings low, dragging on the ground. A wattle may even turn a deeper red as blood rushes to it, which helps attract the attention of hens.

This is called multimodal communication because it combines two kinds of cues—in this case, auditory and visual—to communicate a message. The turkey's message is "I'm a great mate." Multimodal communication increases the chance that the message will be received even if there are distractions or disturbances nearby.

INSIDER INFO

A TURKEY HAS A WATTLE, skin that hangs down from its lower jaw, and a comb, which is the growth on the top of its head. It also has a snood, which is the flap of skin that hangs over its beak. These features, as well as the turkey's feet, keep it cool because the bare skin is exposed directly to air, while the rest of its body is covered with warm feathers.

MALE TURKEYS **POOP** IN THE SHAPE OF A J, AND FEMALES **POOP** IN A **SPIRAL** SHAPE.

DONKEYS ARE PACK ANIMALS, WHICH MEANS THEY CAN CARRY HEAVY ITEMS—AS MUCH AS TWICE THEIR OWN BODY WEIGHT.

Hey! I'm talking to you!

DONKEY

LOCATION: DESERTS, SAVANNAS

PRIMARY COMMUNICATION: 👂 👁 ✋

Donkeys communicate through braying. A bray is when they breathe in to make a *hee* then breath out to make a *haw*. Every donkey brays in its own unique style. Some donkeys bray quietly, while others make a thunderous noise. Donkeys also snort, as a warning alarm. Grunts and growls are used to get the attention of other donkeys.

In addition to verbal cues, donkeys communicate with body language. Donkeys naturally freeze in place when they feel scared or threatened. This is as if they are trying to say, "I'm not going any farther." That same stance is also a way they can use their posture to show confidence. It's a message that means something like "I'm not going away."

The position of a donkey's ears (perked up or flattened back) and tail (relaxed or swishing) as well as the position of its body can tell you a lot about what a donkey is trying to communicate. If a donkey turns around and presents its rear end, that's a sign that it's upset. It's best to step back because a forceful kick is one way it expresses anger. This kicking can get violent, especially if a donkey detects its baby is in danger.

All horse relatives, including donkeys, have hairs on their face that can sense touch and vibrations. Donkeys greet each other by rubbing noses and smelling each other.

INSIDER INFO

DONKEYS GET ALONG WELL with many other animals, including horses, cows, goats, and llamas. They are also used as companion animals for young horses, injured and recovering animals, and even humans. According to experts, their presence can be calming to anxious adults, kids, and animals. They're often referred to as "big dogs," because—just like dogs—they can be friendly and soothing.

COW

LOCATION: PLAINS

PRIMARY COMMUNICATION:

Sure, we all know that a cow says "moo." But we've learned not all moos sound alike. In fact, each moo sends a very different message. A mother cow makes a low sound when her calf (baby cow) is near and a higher sound when the calf is farther away. The calf makes a call to its mother when it's lost or when it wants to eat. The sounds are specific to each mother and baby so that they can recognize each other's voices. That's important because cows mostly live in herds where there could be many mothers and calves mooing at the same time.

Cows also moo when they are looking for a mate or as a warning call if a predator is nearby. Grunting is another way that cows communicate. They may make a contented-sounding grunt while they are eating or grunt more forcefully to show that their rank is higher than another cow's. As with many other animals, the position of a cow's ears is also a signal. You can tell whether a cow is relaxed or stressed by whether its ears are in a natural position or are flattened backward.

Say What? A COW HAS FOUR stomachs—or rather, one stomach divided into four pouches. It barely chews its food before swallowing it. The food travels to the first stomach. Once that stomach is full, the food is pushed back up into the cow's mouth, and it chews it again. This is called "chewing cud." There's so much work involved in digesting the food that cows spend eight hours of their day chomping.

DR. WILD'S WORDS MOTHER COWS AND THEIR BABIES RECOGNIZE EACH OTHER by their moo. Cows are extremely social creatures that have an individual, unique voice for when they are about to be fed, when they're denied food, or when they feel isolated within their herd. Scientists believe other cows can therefore recognize their friends' "voices" by their moo.

EASTERN COTTONTAIL

THE WORLD'S **LARGEST RABBIT** BREED IS THE FLEMISH GIANT RABBIT, WHICH CAN **GROW** TO BE 2.5 FEET (0.8 M) LONG AND **WEIGH** 22 POUNDS (10 KG).

FLEMISH GIANT

RABBIT

LOCATION: MEADOWS, FORESTS, DESERTS, WETLANDS, GRASSLANDS

PRIMARY COMMUNICATION: 👂 👃 👁

*T*hump, thump, thump. That must be the sound of a rabbit. But only a few rabbit species, including brush rabbits and cottontails, thump the ground with their back feet. This thumping noise is not a happy one. It's a signal to other rabbits that a human, squirrel, owl, or other predator is near. Rabbits also wave their white tails as a quiet warning flag. When they want to attack, they'll lower their ears, lift their head up, and lunge forward.

For the most part, rabbits are silent creatures. But they can make vocalizations. If caught by a predator, they scream a high-pitched call that means "Help!" They growl when they feel threatened—and they might bite. They hiss at other rabbits that they don't like. If they purr like a cat, it means "I'm content." But this noise isn't really a vocalization—it's made by rubbing their teeth together.

Rabbits have scent glands on their cheeks and chin. They rub those scents onto their furry coat while they are grooming themselves. These scents can attract other rabbits, tell rabbits what their rank is, and mark their territory—that's a way of saying to other rabbits, "This is mine."

INSIDER INFO

WHAT'S THE DIFFERENCE BETWEEN A RABBIT AND A HARE? Hares are larger, have longer ears, and can run longer distances. They also live aboveground. Rabbits are smaller and are built to run in shorter bursts. They live underground in burrows. Another difference: Hares usually live alone, while rabbits live in groups of up to 20 that are called colonies.

HARE

CAT

LOCATION: URBAN AREAS, GRASSLANDS, FORESTS

PRIMARY COMMUNICATION: 👁 👂 👃

You might assume that cats meow at each other to communicate. But the truth is that adult cats meow only to humans. A meow means they want to say hello, they need something, or they want to let us know that something is wrong. Kittens do meow to their mothers if they're cold or hungry. But once a cat grows up, it stops meowing at other cats. Instead, to get another cat's attention it will yowl.

Cats have a lot to say to each other—and they don't even have to make a noise to say it. Their body language expresses so much. A cat can rotate its ears 180 degrees from facing forward, which means it is content, to flattened, which means it is scared. When a cat's ears are flattened, its whiskers backward, its tail straight, and its back arched, the cat is angry or upset.

When a cat is relaxed, it purrs and might knead its paws on a surface. An angry cat growls, hisses, and sometimes spits. A cat marks its territory in multiple ways. It may pee on the ground or "spray," which is when it backs up to a vertical surface with a raised tail and pees on it. Both are a way of saying, "This is mine. Stay out!" But it can also send a more relaxed territorial message by rubbing its body against something or scratching something. A cat has scent glands on its ears, the back of its head, its neck, and its claws. A cat's nose is 30 times more sensitive than a human's nose, so it can pick up a lot of smells.

CATS ARE **FARSIGHTED,** WHICH MEANS THINGS WITHIN **TWO FEET** (0.6 M) OF THEIR EYES LOOK **BLURRY.**

HORSES CAN **SLEEP** **LYING DOWN** OR **STANDING UP.**

Hay, friend!

HORSE

LOCATION: SHRUBLANDS, PLAINS, HIGHLANDS

PRIMARY COMMUNICATION: 👁 👂

Horses can swivel their ears almost 180 degrees—and they use these wiggly ears as a way to communicate. They can also point their ears up in attention or lay them flat when they are nervous, angry, or afraid. When they are relaxed, their ears relax in the middle. The position of their ears as well as the direction of their gaze send messages to other horses about the location of food (such as grasses) or predators (such as wolves or mountain lions). If one horse's body language points toward a certain direction, other horses will take note and also look that way.

You can guess a horse's emotion by studying its face. Facial gestures like head bobbing or "smiling," when a horse raises its lips to expose teeth, mean that a horse is content. A raised head and neck position means a horse is at attention, or may sense danger nearby and may flee. If the whites of the horse's eyes are showing, it means it is very afraid.

In addition to gestures, horses vocalize when they want to express a feeling. A low neigh or a whinny is a friendly greeting. A soft nicker is used by a mother horse to greet her foals. And a snort is an alarm bell that warns other horses that danger is nearby. If a horse is lost, it will give a high-pitched neigh to say, "Where are you?" The rest of the herd will whinny back to say, "Over here." Male horses neigh to females that they admire. And they grunt, squeal, or scream at males they don't like. They may also bite, kick, or arch their neck as if to say, "Get away."

DR. WILD'S WORDS

HORSES SEEM TO UNDERSTAND HUMAN forms of communication by reading facial emotions. In general, horses respond calmly and more positively to people who are smiling and are more cautious around people with frowns. But that's not all! They even remember the particular emotional expressions of those people.

HARVEST MICE

Mice of you to drop by!

MICE BELONG TO THE ORDER OF ANIMALS CALLED RODENTIA, WHICH FORM NEARLY HALF OF ALL PLACENTAL MAMMALS—SOME 2,277 SPECIES!

MOUSE

LOCATION: WORLDWIDE EXCEPT ANTARCTICA

PRIMARY COMMUNICATION: 🦻 👁 👃

Mice make about 20 different kinds of vocalizations to express their emotions. But humans can't hear them all because the squeaks they make are ultrasonic, meaning the sound waves are too high for humans to pick up. Did you know that mice bark at each other when they are angry? Short tweets and yelps are used for friendlier vocalization. Some calls are more complicated: A male mouse will "sing" a complex song to a female when he wants to impress her.

They also use body language to communicate. Mice rattle their tails when they are angry. When deer mice feel threatened, they drum their paws on the ground quickly as a warning signal to let others know that trouble is near.

Mice have one more form of communication—through pee. One mouse can smell another mouse's urine and learn a lot. It can tell if the mouse is male or female, whether it's from the same species of mice or a different one, and what its rank is and whether it is dominant or submissive. The scent can also mark their territory, which reminds other mice to back off.

INSIDER INFO

MICE USE WHISKERS TO NAVIGATE THEIR ENVIRONMENT. (They can't see well.) It's similar to the way humans use their fingers to feel around a dark room to figure out where objects are located. Each of a mouse's 24 whiskers can sense what's around. Then its brain creates a "map" of what the space looks like. As the mouse moves its head, the map changes.

LLAMA

LOCATION: MOUNTAINS

PRIMARY COMMUNICATION: 👂 👁

Mother llamas hum to their babies, called cria. The crias hum back, which is their first step in communicating with each other. This is important because mothers and babies recognize each other by their hums. Llamas communicate with other vocalizations, too.

INSIDER INFO

BOTH LLAMAS AND ALPACAS are a part of the camelid family, and it can be hard to tell them apart. There are some differences: Llamas have long ears and long snouts, while alpacas have short ears and shorter snouts. Easy, right?

ALPACA

Male llamas send a warning call to alert everyone when a predator is near. Other male llamas in the area will start repeating the call to make sure everyone hears it. Males also scream when they fight and make a gargling noise called an orgle when they like a female.

In the wild, llamas live in groups of up to 20, but only one male llama can be dominant, or the leader. To defend his position as top llama, he may stand on higher ground to show he's more dominant than other llamas. He will even fight other llamas if necessary. His body language (such as wrapping his long neck around another llama or biting another llama's neck) is a way of saying, "Let's fight." The two llamas will try to wrestle each other to the ground and whichever one falls first is the loser. The loser will say, "I give up" by using body language: He lies on his side with his neck lowered and his tail raised.

When it's time to protect themselves or tell a predator to "Get away," llamas spit, kick, bite, and charge. Although they are very protective of their space, llamas have been known to take in sheep as members of their own family and protect them.

LLAMAS CAN **RUN** AS **FAST** AS **35 MILES** AN HOUR (56 KM/H).

DR. WILD'S WORDS

A CAMELID (ALPACAS, CAMELS, LLAMAS, GUANACO, AND VICUÑAS) can really let you know when they don't want you around. They either kick, headbutt, or spit. But there is a trick to knowing when one is about to spit. You'll see the lower eyelid turn outward (something us veterinarians call "ectropion"), creating a "worry wrinkle." Then you might notice the camelid tightening up its lips. Its ears lie back, it lifts its head, and then—wham!—it hurls a spitball toward your face.

GOAT MILK IS EASIER FOR HUMANS TO DIGEST THAN **COW MILK.**

GOAT

LOCATION: WORLDWIDE EXCEPT ANTARCTICA

PRIMARY COMMUNICATION:

There are only a few animal species in the world that gaze at humans when they need help. Dogs do it. Horses do, too. And so do goats. That's probably because, like dogs and horses, goats have been living near humans for thousands of years. This gaze is one way that goats have learned how to communicate.

The most common way goats send messages to each other is through bleating, which is a *mahhh*-like noise that can sometimes sound like a human screaming. Goat babies, called kids, can recognize their mother's bleat immediately after birth. Mother goats call to the kids to keep them near. These are called contact calls.

Goats also communicate with chemical cues. Male goats make a scent that tells the other goats their rank. Only one male goat can be the leader of the group. If a goat disagrees with who is the most dominant, the leader might use body language to prove his point. Male goats can butt heads with their spiral horns as a way to fight and show who is strongest. But at other times they use this kind of body language to simply play.

Say What? GOATS WALK ON ONLY TWO OF THEIR FOUR TOES, but they have incredible balance. They can climb trees and walk on ledges as thin as a tightrope. They also can jump as high as five feet (1.5 m). The bottom of each of their hooves is very soft, which allows them to grip surfaces.

NOT HORSIN' AROUND

Scientists rave about dogs, dolphins, and apes and their abilities to communicate with humans. But horse lovers know that their equine pals are quite intelligent, too. Horses can learn tricks that help them communicate with humans. They can go so far as to gesture to humans to express their feelings.

One trainer in Norway taught horses how to express to humans whether they were hot or cold. The horses touched their muzzle to a board with symbols. The symbols stood for "blanket on," "blanket off," or "no change." It took only two weeks for 23 horses to learn this skill. From then on, the horses could let their trainer know what they preferred. This behavior is much more than performing a trick—it's communication.

Horses have also been known to "point" to objects that they want. One study put buckets of oats, apples, and carrots on the other side of a fence. A human stood nearby but did nothing. The horses would gaze longingly at the food and then at the human. Once they made eye contact with the human, the horse would nod its head quickly toward the bucket it wanted. The horse made noises and movements to get the human's attention and then draw that human's attention to the other side of the fence. This is called referential communication. It means that a gesture is given (the horse nods) to direct the attention of someone (the human) toward a goal (the bucket of food).

Horses are known to recognize humans' facial expressions (happy versus angry) and body language, such as pointing to a bucket. But some scientists believe that many horses have stopped trying to communicate with us because we don't listen. When horses can add meaning to actions through observation and experience (instead of just memorizing a command), there's a better chance that our two species will be able to understand each other.

A HORSE TOUCHING ITS MUZZLE TO A BOARD TO COMMUNICATE WITH HUMANS

THIS HORSE IS LETTING ITS HANDLERS KNOW IF IT WANTS A BLANKET PUT ON OR TAKEN OFF, OR TO STAY UNCHANGED.

QUIZ: WHAT IS THIS ANIMAL SAYING?

Learn how well you understand animals by answering the questions below. All of the answers can be found earlier in this book.

1 When a cat flattens its ears and whiskers backward, straightens its tail, and arches its back, that cat is ...

    A. excited.

    B. angry.

    C. tired.

2 If a donkey turns around and presents its rear end, it means ...

    A. it's about to run the other way.

    B. kicking with its back legs will likely follow.

    C. it's bored.

3 Which animal makes a sound called bleating?

    A. a gerbil

    B. a turkey

    C. a goat

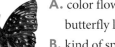

4 The different colors and patterns of a butterfly's wings tell what ...

A. color flowers the butterfly likes to eat.

B. kind of species the butterfly is.

C. time of day the butterfly sleeps.

5 Spiders use their webs to learn information by ...

A. feeling vibrations in the web's silk.

B. observing the world below from high up in their web.

C. inviting other spiders to hang out and chat.

6 If an elephant lifts a leg, flaps its ears, and makes a rumble, it's likely saying:

A. "Let's go this way."

B. "Predator ahead."

C. "Do you smell what I'm smelling?"

7 Scientists originally thought only land-dwelling tortoises could make noise, but recently discovered that baby sea turtles also make what kind of noises?

A. whistles and barks

B. clicks, hoots, and clucks

C. squeaks and chirps

8 Which animals exchange information by creating a giant shared pile of poop?

A. rhinoceros

B. prairie dogs

C. bats

9 When a hedgehog tucks itself into a ball, it's saying:

A. "Let's play!"

B. "Don't eat me."

C. "Whee! Let's go for a roll."

10 If a male eagle flies high in the air, folds his wings, then drops headfirst, it means he's ...

A. escaping from a predator.

B. getting ready to hunt.

C. trying to impress a female.

ANSWERS: 1. B; 2. B; 3. C; 4. B; 5. A; 6. A; 7. B; 8. A; 9. B; 10. C.

GLOSSARY

appeasement: to bring to a calm and peaceful state

appendage: a projecting part of an organism with a distinct function, such as an arm or a leg

auditory: relating to hearing, sounds, or vocalizations

biofluorescence: a process where an animal's skin absorbs light and reemits it as a different color

bioluminescence: a chemical process that creates light energy within the body of an organism

buoyant: having the ability to float

camouflage: an animal's coloring that lets it blend into its surroundings

chemical communication: a process by which animals communicate through pheromones in a way that affects the behavior of another animal

chemoreception: a process where organisms respond to chemical cues, often through taste or smell

chemotactic sense: the movement an animal makes (toward or away) after sensing a chemical signal

choreography: a sequence of movements or steps

communication: the exchanging of information

diapause: the insect term for hibernation

domesticated: a term used to describe animals that have been tamed and adapted for human use, such as pets or farm animals

dominant: more powerful, or the highest position or rank

duet: a song and/or dance performance by two life-forms

echolocation: the process by which objects are located through the reflection of sound

facial expression: the way you arrange the features of your face to communicate

fluke: the two fins of a whale's tail

gesture: a way you communicate using your hands or limbs

heterospecific: when an organism belongs to a different species or group

hibernation: the period of time in which an animal remains dormant, or inactive, during the winter season

intruder: an uninvited and unwanted guest

language: a method of communication that can be spoken, signed, or written

migrate: a process by which an animal moves from one region to another seasonally

nesting: the process by which a bird builds or occupies a nest

nocturnal: the state of being most active at night, instead of during the day

offspring: an animal's young

pheromones: the chemicals an animal emits that affect the behavior of another animal

pigment: the natural coloring that makes up an animal or plant

pollinator: anything that helps move pollen from the male part of a flower to the female part of a flower; for example, a honeybee

posture: the position of your body parts when you sit or stand

predator: an animal that preys on other animals

prey: an animal that is hunted by others

regenerate: to regrow or replace

social: prefers to spend time around others

solitary: prefers to exist alone

stridulation: when an insect rubs parts of its body together to produce a sound

submissive: less powerful, submitting to the will of others

subordinate: a lower rank or position

symbiotic: a relationship between two organisms that benefits, or helps, both of them at the same time

syntax: how words are arranged to form a sentence

tactile: relating to touching

talon: a bird's claw

territorial: protecting your home from unwanted guests

ultrasonic: sound waves that are too high for a human to hear

ultraviolet: meaning "beyond violet," electromagnetic radiation that sits beyond the spectrum of light visible to humans at its violet end

urine: also known as pee, a watery waste fluid that's stored in the bladder of living organisms

visual: relating to seeing

vocalization: the process of making sounds with your voice

RESOURCES

BOOKS

Absolute Expert: Dolphins
Jennifer Swanson and Justine Jackson-Ricketts, National Geographic Books, 2018

Everything Birds of Prey
Blake Hoena, National Geographic Books, 2015

Everything Predators
Blake Hoena, National Geographic Books, 2016

Fetch!
A How to Speak Dog Training Guide
Aubre Andrus and Gary Weitzman, D.V.M.,
National Geographic Books, 2020

How to Speak Dog:
A Guide to Decoding Dog Language
Aline Alexander Newman and Gary Weitzman, D.V.M., National Geographic Books, 2013

How to Speak Cat:
A Guide to Decoding Cat Language
Aline Alexander Newman and Gary Weitzman, D.V.M., National Geographic Books, 2015

National Geographic Animal Encyclopedia, 2nd ed.
National Geographic Books, 2021

Ocean Animals:
Who's Who in the Deep Blue
Johnna Rizzo, National
Geographic Books, 2016

Pounce!
A How to Speak Cat Training Guide
Tracey West and Gary Weitzman,
D.V.M., National Geographic
Books, 2020

Ultimate Bugopedia
Darlyne Murawski and Nancy
Honovich, National Geographic
Books, 2013

Ultimate Explorer Field Guide:
Reptiles and Amphibians
Catherine Herbert Howell, National
Geographic Books, 2016

Ultimate Oceanpedia
Christina Wilsdon, National
Geographic Books, 2016

Ultimate Predatorpedia
Christina Wilsdon, National
Geographic Books, 2018

Ultimate Reptileopedia
Christina Wilsdon, National
Geographic Books, 2015

Wild Vet Adventures:
Saving Animals Around the World
With Dr. Gabby Wild
Gabby Wild and Jennifer Szymanski,
National Geographic Books, 2021

WEBSITES
A note for parents and teachers: For more
information on this topic, you can visit
these websites with your young readers.

National Geographic
kids.nationalgeographic.com

Ranger Rick
https://rangerrick.org

San Diego Zoo
kids.sandiegozoowildlifealliance.org

Smithsonian's National Zoo and
Conservation Biology Institute
https://nationalzoo.si.edu

ZooBorns
https://www.zooborns.com

See you later!

INDEX

PHOTO CREDITS

AS: Adobe Stock; ASP: Alamy Stock Photo; GI: Getty Images; MP: Minden Pictures; NGIC: National Geographic Image Collection; NGP: National Geographic Partners; SS: Shutterstock

COVER: Front (UP LE), Daniel Prudek/SS; (UP RT), Kurit afshen/SS; (LO LE), Mayskyphoto/SS; (LO RT), kyslynskahal/SS; Back (LE), Sonsedska Yuliia/SS; (RT), Dirk Ercken/SS; Spine, Eric Isselee/SS; **FRONT MATTER:** 2-3, NataSnow/SS; 4, Štěpán Kápl/AS; 4-5, Alexander Potapov/AS; 5, Dennis Von Linden/SS; 8, Rebecca Hale/National Geographic Staff; **CHAPTER 1:** 10 (LE), Vladimir Seliverstov/Dreamstime; 10 (RT), Raymond Gehman/NGIC; 11 (UP LE), Thomas Marent/MP; 11 (UP RT), Ibrahim Suha Derbent/Photodisc; 11 (LO LE), Mitchell Krog/GI; 11 (LO RT), Guan Jiangchi/AS; 12-13, kali9/E+/GI; 14, Hung Chung Chih/SS; 15 (UP LE), Ger Bosma/Moment/GI; 15 (UP RT), Mohd Khairi Ibrahim/Dreamstime; 15 (LO LE), Tom & Pat Leeson/ARDEA; 15 (LO RT), Karoline Thalhofer/AS; 17, kyslynskahal/AS; 18, Pixie Chick/AS; 20, Rod Planck/Science Source; 21, Henk Bentlage/SS; 22, Stan Tekielar/Moment/GI; 23, MZ Photo/SS; 25, Photo Attractive/E+/GI; **CHAPTER 2:** 26-27, Mark O'Flaherty/SS; 28, Jak Wonderly/NGP; 29 (UP), Konrad Wothe/MP; 29 (CTR), Joseph Van Os/Stockbyte/GI; 29 (LO), Jurgen and Christine Sohns/MP; 30, Tetra Images/David Arky/Brand X Pictures/GI; 31, Supakrit Tirayasupasin/Moment/GI; 32, blickwinkel/ASP; 33 (LE), Dennis Donohue/AS; 33 (RT), Joao Burini/MP; 34 (LE), I. Pilon/AS; 34 (RT), PetrP/SS; 35, Premaphotos/MP; 36-37, Okan/AS; 38, Joel Sartore/NGIC; 39, gator/AS; 40 (UP), Wanchai Chaipanya/Dreamstime; 40 (LO), Natthawut/AS; 41, Papilio/ASP; 42, Manoj Shah/GI; 43, Pete Oxford/MP; 44, Matthijs Kuijpers/ASP; 45 (UP), Jak Wonderly/NGP; 45 (LO), Ken Griffiths/ASP; 46, Van Truan/AS; 47, Roberto/AS; 48, Ignacio Palacios/Stone/GI; 49, pirotehnik/AS; 50, Gary K Smith/ASP; 51 (UP), John Porter LRPS/ASP; 51 (LO), Barry Mansell/MP; 52, Alex Hibbert/The Image Bank/GI; 52, NBC Newswire/NBC Universal/GI; 54, Terry Allen/AS; 55 (UP), Donald M. Jones/MP; 55 (LO), Scott Suriano/Moment/GI; 56, WL Davies/E+/GI; 57, Santanu Nandy/Moment Open/GI; 58, michaklootwijk/AS; 59, Teguh Santosa/Moment/GI; 60, so3media/AS; 61, Mitsuaki Iwago/MP; 62, AnneGM/AS; 62-63, Panu Ruangjan/SS; 65 (UP), AP Photo; 65 (LO), Ronald H. Cohn/NGIC; **CHAPTER 3:** 66-67, Gallo Images/Brand X Pictures/GI; 68, James R.D. Scott/Moment/GI; 69, tubuceo/SS; 70, Tom McHugh/Science Source; 71, Corey Douglas/U.S. Fish & Wildlife Service; 72, Mathieu Meur/Stocktrek Images/GI; 73, A. Martin UW Photography/GI; 74, kavram/SS; 75, Reinhold Leitner/SS; 76, Richard Carey/Dreamstime; 76-77, Gerard Lacz/FLPA/MP; 78, FluxFactory/GI; 79, Sanamyan/ASP; 80, Avalon.red/ASP; 81, Rich Carey/SS; 82, Paulo de Oliveira/Biosphoto/MP; 83, Masa Ushioda/Blue Planet Archive; 84, Hotshotsworldwide/Dreamstime; 85, Elliott Neep/MP; 86 (UP), Subphoto/AS; 86 (LO), Tobias Bernhard/GI; 87, Steve Azer/AS; 88, Pär Edlund/Dreamstime; 89, Gudkov Andrey/SS; 90, Joao Pedro Silva/SS; 91, Georgette Douwma/Nature Picture Library; 92 (UP), KeithSzafranski/GI; 92 (LO), Sergey/AS; 93, Foto Mous/SS; 95 (UP), Robert Smith/SS; 95 (LO), Michael Zeigler/E+/GI; 96, Lotus41/Moment/GI; 97, whitcomberd/AS; 98, Bob Gibbons/FLPA/MP; 99, Kevin Pronnecke/GI; 100, Linda Lewis/FLPA/MP; 101, George Grall/NGIC; 102 (UP), Nick Dale/500px Plus/GI; 102 (LO), Grispb/AS; 103, donyanedomam/AS; 105 (UP), Ed Kashi/Hulton Archive/GI; 105 (LO), Brian Skerry/NGIC; **CHAPTER 4:** 106-107, Alan Murphy/MP; 108 (UP), Ongushi/AS; 108 (LO), Mikael Damkier/Dreamstime; 109, Victor Tyakht/AS; 110, Danita Delimont/SS; 111, Chien Lee/MP; 112, Satoshi Kuribayashi/Nature Production/MP; 113, Chandrashan Perera/ASP; 114, santa2030/GI; 115, Edwin Giesbers/Nature Picture Library; 116, Nicholas Bergkessel Jr./Science Source; 117, S&D&K Maslowski/FLPA/MP; 118, PIXATERRA/AS; 119 (UP), Andre Skonieczny/GI; 119 (LO), David/AS; 120, Dennis Von Linden/SS; 121, Judit Dombovari/ASP; 122 (UP), Markus Varesvuo/Nature Picture Library; 122, Ivan/AS; 123, Bob Gibbons/ASP; 124-125, Peter Fleming/AS; 125, Henrik Larsson/SS; 126 (LE), Hal Beral/Corbis/GI; 126 (RT), Daybreak Imagery/ASP; 127, ondrejprosicky/AS; 128, Julian Kaesler/Moment/GI; 129, Annette Scholtz; 130, Sia Kambou/AFP/GI; 131, hugh sturrock/ASP; 132 (UP), Paul Reeves/iStockPhoto; 132 (LO), Hiroyuki Uchiyama/Moment Open/GI; 133, Vicki Jauron/Babylon and Beyond Photography/Moment/GI; 134-135, Martin Willis/MP; 135, Gianpiero Ferrari/FLPA/MP; 136, Kevin Hellon/SS; 137, Michael Quinton/MP; 138-139, Anacleto Rapping/Los Angeles Times/GI; **CHAPTER 5:** 140-141, Clara/AS; 142 (UP), S Quintans/AS; 142 (LO), ARTSILENSE/SS; 143, Monkey Business/AS; 144, jadimages/SS; 145, talseN/SS; 146, Juniors Bildarchiv GmbH/ASP; 147, Camilo Torres/SS; 148, photomaster/SS; 149, Donald M. Jones/MP; 150, Buena Vista Images/Stone/GI; 151, Stefania Besca/Moment Open/GI; 152, Dave Pressland/FLPA/MP; 153, Design Pics/GI; 154 (UP), Chris_timachai/SS; 154 (LO), Bonita/AS; 155, Volodymyr Byrdyak/Dreamstime; 156, Life On White/Photodisc/GI; 157, Syda Productions/AS; 158, putzlowitsch/AS; 159, Igor Alecsander/E+/GI; 160, Andy Sands/Nature Picture Library; 161, Anneke/AS; 162, Gannet77/E+/GI; 163, Ines Meier/AS; 165, MarkLG1973/AS; 167 (BOTH), Mejdell CM, Buvik T, Jørgensen GHM, Bøe KE. Applied Animal Behaviour Science 2016, 184: 66-73.; 168-169, Butterfly Hunter/SS; 168 (LO LE), Paolo Gallo/EyeEm/GI; 168 (LO RT), Gunter/AS; 169, Eric Isselee/SS; 172-173, Anton Rodionov/SS

To everyone who chooses zoolingualism as their superpower.
—Aubre Andrus

Since 1888, the National Geographic Society has funded more than 14,000 research, conservation, education, and storytelling projects around the world. National Geographic Partners distributes a portion of the funds it receives from your purchase to National Geographic Society to support programs including the conservation of animals and their habitats. To learn more, visit natgeo.com/info.

For more information, visit nationalgeographic.com, call 1-877-873-6846, or write to the following address:

National Geographic Partners, LLC
1145 17th Street NW
Washington, DC 20036-4688 U.S.A.

For librarians and teachers: nationalgeographic.com/books/librarians-and-educators

More for kids from National Geographic: natgeokids.com

National Geographic Kids magazine inspires children to explore their world with fun yet educational articles on animals, science, nature, and more. Using fresh storytelling and amazing photography, *Nat Geo Kids* shows kids ages 6 to 14 the fascinating truth about the world—and why they should care. **natgeo.com/subscribe**

For rights or permissions inquiries, please contact National Geographic Books Subsidiary Rights: bookrights@natgeo.com

Designed by Brett Challos

Library of Congress Cataloging-in-Publication Data

Names: Andrus, Aubre, author. | Wild, Gabby, author.
Title: How to speak animal : a guide to learning how animals communicate / Aubre Andrus and Dr. Gabby Wild, D.V.M.
Description: Washington, D.C. : National Geographic Kids, [2022] | Includes index. | Audience: Ages 8-12 | Audience: Grades 4-6 |
Identifiers: LCCN 2021023112 | ISBN 9781426372384 (trade paperback) | ISBN 9781426372391 (library binding)
Subjects: LCSH: Animal communication--Juvenile literature.
Classification: LCC QL776 .A525 2022 | DDC 591.59--dc23
LC record available at https://lccn.loc.gov/2021023112

Acknowledgments
Thank you to all those who dedicate their lives to better understanding our furry friends. The publisher would like to thank Erica Jacobs Green, project editor; Ariane Szu-Tu, senior editor; Michaela Weglinski, assistant editor; Lori Epstein, photo director; Nicole DiMella, photo editor; Jennifer Geddes, fact-checker; and Anne LeongSon and Gus Tello, associate designers.

Printed in China
22/PPS/1